When I Need God the Most

Finding His Help When Life Gets Tense and Tough

H. Curtis McDaniel

PRESS

Xulon Press
11350 Random Hill Center
Suite 800
Fairfax, VA 22030
(703) 279-6511
XulonPress.com

DEDICATION

This book is lovingly dedicated to some special people in my life who taught me in one way or another many of the truths you will read in the following pages.

- My wife Karen who shows me regularly what trusting God looks like in daily living;
- My children Curtis, Megan and Heather who remind me that the principles of God's Word can make a profound difference in life when they are learned and applied early;
- My mother Velma "Babs" McDaniel and my departed father, the late Curtis McDaniel, Sr., who reared me to understand and to embrace many of the truths taught in these chapters;
- My childhood Sunday School teachers in West End Presbyterian Church in Hopewell, Virginia who taught me each Sunday to love the Lord and to honor His Word in my life;
- My dear friends Mr. and Mrs. William J. Gordy (Bill and Betty) of Montgomery, Alabama who model the truths of these principles by their life;
- And to my dear departed friend, the Honorable Judge Joseph David Phelps who exemplified in his humble life what God can do when someone fully trusts Him.

Since the pages of this work reflect your investment in my life, may the Holy Spirit multiply your influence to touch many people to turn to the Lord where they will find grace, truth, strength and wisdom when they need Him the most.

I want to thank sincerely my sister-in-law Diane Preston for her careful and good editing of this work.

May Christ be honored.

H. Curtis McDaniel
November 2001

INTRODUCTION

GOD, I REALLY NEED YOU

On a Friday afternoon more than halfway through my first semester in seminary, I was taking a major language exam when one of the most significant bookmarks in my life happened. I noticed throughout the test period that several library assistants kept coming into the classroom quietly and whispering words to my professor. I looked up one time and noticed that they were staring at me. "I wonder why they're looking at me," I thought. But the intensity of the hour drove me to focus on my exam with undivided concentration. I wanted to do well and to finish the test with confidence and clarity.

As was my usual custom, I was the last person to turn in the exam. Teachers always taught us to review our answers, then recheck them to make sure there were no mistakes. I turned the test over, placed it on the professor's desk and walked out the door. No sooner than I exited the room than my professor met me and asked if he could speak to me privately. I'd never experienced this before, so I said, "yes" with an air of tension.

We walked into an adjacent vacant classroom were he looked at me and said, "Have you heard anything today?" I told him I didn't know what he meant. He said, "You know, is anything on your mind? Have you heard from home?" I replied, "No, not for a couple of days. The last time I called home was last Sunday to wish my dad a happy birthday."

Then he broke the word to me. "I'm sorry to be the bearer of sad news but your father died this morning in his sleep." When he said it, I fell into a state of shock and numbness. I couldn't believe what I was hearing. The man who loved me more than his own life had departed this world to be in the presence of the Lord.

I thought it would never happen, but it did. For a number of weeks, I lived in a state of grief, regularly praying, "God are you there? *I really need You now more than ever.* Do you have any help to give me? My road is really rough now. Will you come near me?"

I found from that experience and from many others in my life that God specializes in helping us when we need Him the most. When confusion, worry, fear, family, the future, marriage, work and finances trouble our spirits, God has significant wisdom to offer us so that we can be equipped to handle these issues in our lives.

But God doesn't put us through these experiences in a vacuum. The Lord teaches us lessons from those times so that we can help others when they experience trouble in their lives. *When I Need God the Most* is an effort to look at some of the most common troubles that people experience in their daily lives on an introductory level. Chances are good that if you're struggling with worry, you're also grappling with guidance, money, confusion and discouragement. My prayer is that this book will give you some practical biblical help that can get you started back on the road to hope and personal peace with God and with yourself.

The *TALK TIME!* Questions at the end of each chapter are geared for Bible study groups, Sunday School classes and account-ability clusters to discuss the principles of each subject in an open, understanding environment. Don't overlook these questions and exercises! They can be the most powerful learning tools in the whole discovery process.

If you're experiencing times of deep frustration and hurt, let the Bible speak to your life issues! God is as relevant now as He was thousands of years ago! Let's go to Him to get the answers for real life!

If any thought or principle in this study helps you and/or others find hope and direction in your journey through the tough times in life, to God be the glory.

H. Curtis McDaniel
October, 2001

CONTENTS

PART 2: GOD'S HELP FOR MY FAMILY LIFE

marriage relationship. The key to success lies in the deliberate intentional actions of both parties.

Once we expose the common misunderstandings about children and child-rearing as well as recognize some of the major factors that make parenting so difficult these days, we can turn to the Scriptures to learn several valuable principles that can help us "train up a child in the way he/she should go."

Jesus wouldn't have spent a great deal of time talking about money without a reason. Therefore, it's important that we gain a biblical understanding about it and the proper way to handle it. After all, He doesn't want you living in bondage.

PART 3: HELP IN THE MIDST OF THE TENSION

Sometimes it's just tough handling the daily pains of life. While you're feeling the pain and paying for these troubles and heartaches, is there something you can claim?

PART 1:

GOD'S HELP FOR MY PERSONAL LIFE

1

WHEN GOD CONFUSES ME

"When I tried to understand all this, it was oppressive to me"
Psalm 73:16

Sometimes things don't make sense. I say that every time I drive past the cross and silk flowers at the foot of the Interstate embankment. They recall a day when my office received a troubling telephone call. About ten o'clock in the morning, a pastor-friend across town phoned to tell me that a member of his church who grew up in our church was killed minutes ago in a car accident. The police were looking for his parents who were members of my church. I remember calling their home, letting the phone ring a dozen times. All of a sudden the father answered. "Larry, is that you?" I asked. "Yes," he responded. "I'm just walking in the house from a round of golf. How's it going?" I paused and said, "Uh, I need to come by and see you. Is that okay?" "Sure, come on over" he said. Then, with everything in me trying to stay composed, I asked, "Larry, has anyone talked to you in the last couple of minutes?" "Why, no," he said. "I've talked to no one. I just came in while the phone was ringing."

When I arrived at Larry's home a few minutes later, I saw the policeman break the news to him and his wife. Their adult son was now dead, leaving behind a wife and a kindergarten-aged son. There's no way I can describe the horror of that event. Several hours later, I walked away from their home, looking up at God and saying, *"WHY?"*

Several years ago, two well-known families in the church were expecting children. For one family, it was their first; for the other, their third. Both couples loved the Lord and demonstrated sincere commitment to Him. Yet for some strange reason, when the heart monitor probes attached to their babies during labor and delivery, no heartbeats were detected. They didn't die because their umbilical cord was wrapped around their neck or because of some other well-known cause. They simply didn't have the breath of God in them. At the funeral of the first baby, I asked God during a time of silent prayer, *"WHY?"* Why this child? Why this family?

Several years ago on Palm Sunday, the South experienced some severe thunderstorms, causing hundreds of tornadoes to touch down. One fell in Goshen, Alabama, upon a Methodist Church. To all who recall what happened, it appeared that this tornado came out of nowhere, destroyed the church, and then lifted back up to the sky. Like many people that day, I saw the news reports and sat there in bewilderment. In my spirit, I was saying to God, *"Why a church? Why not the drug dealer's warehouse on the other side of town?*

I could continue this story line but you get the picture. As you go through life, specific things occur that make our heads spin. We look at God and say,

Why? It doesn't make sense.
God, why do you permit this to happen?
God, I don't understand this!
How could you possibly let this happen?
God, you confuse me!

These feelings summon everything within us in search of an answer. I confess times have come when I felt I couldn't go on in life unless some explanation came for these occurrences. I know it doesn't sound "spiritual," but some days you don't *feel* spiritual, much less want to *think* spiritual. You want some answers to the things that hit your life. And you don't want to wait ten years to get an answer that explains everything with 20/20 spiritual hindsight.

Asaph, the writer of the 73rd Psalm echoes some of these feelings. He looks around and sees things in the world that don't make a great deal of sense. In fact, in verse 21, he says he is grieved and embittered about it. He became confused about the dealings and actions of God like many of us today. In similar ways, we go through times where events around us cause us to question God's sovereignty. Then when we muster enough within us to go to Him for a possible explanation, it appears that He turns His back and leaves us in the dark with no answer.

Some think God owes us an explanation. But the Scriptures don't support that opinion. From time to time, we read words like Proverbs 25:2, *"It is the glory of God to conceal a matter"* and we're confronted with the fact that God isn't in the business of always explaining Himself. Then a word like Isaiah 45:15, *"Truly you are a God who hides Himself"* comes at an inopportune time and you feel like someone is picking a spiritual scab off your soul. And the pain and confusion remain. Why does God confuse me at times? Why doesn't He tell me what I want to know?

Solomon realized the same situation and offers His conclusion in Ecclesiastes 11:5, *"As you do not know the path of the wind or how the body is formed in the womb, so you cannot understand the work of God."* Moses said it this way in Deuteronomy 29:29a, *"the secret things belong to the Lord our God."* There's more in the Bible on this matter than we want to see. But the question remains. How do you deal with this? How do you handle this confusion? Is there a way to comprehend these matters?

LESSON FOCUS

From Psalm 73, we can learn some lessons and valuable perspective when times of confusion come from unexpected events and hardships in our lives. From God's point of view, what we need to learn from those moments is not only to ask Him, *"WHY?"* but also *"WHAT?"* You can gain great strength when you look at the Lord and say, "God, what do you want me to learn about you and this in my life?"

SOMETIMES THINGS DON'T MAKE SENSE

The Psalmist looked around at the things going on in the world in his day and they didn't make sense to him. Right was wrong. Up was down. Truth was inverted. He tried to think it through, reason it out and even look at it from a different perspective. But still it didn't bring satisfaction in his mind. In fact, the *more* he thought about it, the heavier it burdened his spirit. Notice the revealing words of verse 16, *"when I tried to understand all this, it was oppressive to me."* What was bothering him?

· *The first thing that didn't make sense for him was the prosperity of the wicked.* Everywhere he looked, he saw the wrong people gaining the success of the world. You can feel the rub in his spirit as he writes in verse 2,

> *But as for me, my feet had almost slipped; I had nearly lost my foothold. For I envied the arrogant when I saw the prosperity of the wicked. They have no struggles; their bodies are healthy and strong. They are free from the burdens common to man; they are not plagued by human ills.*

We people that fit this description regularly. Like the Psalmist, I can say, "Been there, *seen* that!" Quite a few people over my lifetime have appeared from this category. They have more money than they can possibly spend. They do whatever they want to do, go wherever they want to go and spend their time in self-centered ways. Their pursuits take them on some of the most meaningless treks in life. Yet they love it and laugh at the way others look at them. The Psalmist saw how the wicked lived such a burden-free life, with a carefree and nonchalant attitude toward everything. When he saw this, it was oppressive to him.

The second thing that didn't make sense for him was the agenda of the wicked. When he saw them act and speak in public, he heard arrogance and egotism spew from their mouth. Picture in your mind the portrait he paints of them starting in verse 6:

> *Therefore pride is their necklace; they clothe themselves with violence. From their callous hearts comes iniquity, the evil conceits of their minds know no limits. They scoff, and speak with malice; in their arrogance they threaten oppression. Their mouths lay claim to heaven, and their tongues take possession of the earth.*

It wasn't enough that they adorned themselves with evil attitudes and wicked temperaments. The Psalmist saw that they had an *agenda* in their actions. Their goal was to take possession of the land for the cause of evil.

You don't have to look far to see people with this agenda today. From terrorist groups that attack innocent people to organized evil seeking power, control and fear, these people have one thing in common. They have an agenda. They want their convictions to rule and to dominate the landscape of society today. If someone warns them, they react violently, revealing the callous spirit within. The Psalmist saw how the wicked lived with hate and malice towards everyone who threatened their way of life. When he pondered the way they acted and talked, it was oppressive to him.

The third thing that didn't make sense for him was the following of the wicked. It wasn't enough that people were doing these evil activities. The worse part of this whole ordeal was the people that they took with them on the journey. He saw numbers of men and women rejoicing with these deceitful rulers like cult leaders dancing their flocks to destruction. As they lured others to their side during the journey, they attacked the omniscience of God in the process. While drinking from the abundance provided by their rich commanders, they question with belligerence, *"How can God know? Does the Most High have knowledge?"* (v.11). In their minds, if God *knew* about it, He would *do* something about it. But either He doesn't know about it, doesn't care about it or doesn't have the power to do anything about it. This oppressed the Psalmist. He didn't understand. These things burdened and grieved him, making him senseless and embittered (vs. 21-22) the more he thought about it.

These things make us grieve and hurt, too. Anyone that has a heart for God wants to see His glory cover the earth (Habakkuk 2:14). But honesty must confess something at this point. We've all asked Him, "Lord why is this going on? Why do you permit this? Why are you confusing me? You have the power to do something for good. Why don't you *DO* it!?"

WHERE HE LEARNS THE LESSONS

From a worldly perspective, everything the Psalmist saw was in a state of disarray. Everywhere he looked, questions abounded. Things appeared to be turned inside out. He tried to keep his heart pure in the midst of this perplexity, but the more he tried to live for God, the more punishment he received from the enemy (v. 14). Then the thought came to him, *"why not go to God's house for an answer"* (v. 17). So He went to the sanctuary in search of some needed answers. He wanted the pieces of the puzzle connected.

I love verse 17. It puts it into perspective. It says that he didn't understand these things *"till he entered the sanctuary of God."* That comforts! When you stop looking at things from your point of view and start focusing on things from God's point of view, you begin to see why God does what He does. Confusion comes when you try to apply the world's logic and rationale apart from the truth of God's revelation. You get answers to life's difficult issues when you take time to come into God's presence to see His perspective on the issue. Don't expect to understand the way the world is running apart from the wisdom of God. Your head will swirl in bewilderment. You can only find the answers when you enter the sanctuary of God's presence and gather His outlook as you worship Him and study His Word.

This principle doesn't stop with receiving God's perspective to answer these troubling issues. Notice *where* he gained divine perspective. He found it in God's house, probably during worship and from the teaching of the Law. Truth came clearly from God's dwelling place. The lesson is compelling. If you are looking for real answers to the issues you face, seek God in His house for worship. Join other professing believers in regular worship and study of God's Word.

Do you make weekly public worship a regular part of your schedule? As a pastor, few things in life bring me more disappointment than to watch the low priority many professing believers give to faithful, regular attendance at public worship services. You see many of them in hot pursuit of the material things in life, driving them out of town consistently month after month. Then, all of a sudden, something goes wrong in their life and they come back to the church, asking numerous questions in an attempt to patch up their problems. I've seen this more times than I can remember. Time after time, if they would only place a priority on worship, some of the problems they encounter would never come. Why? Because they would have God's perspective for living, helping them to make decisions that would keep them from many of the problems they face in the world. Worship brings the proper fear of the Lord, and the Bible says, *"the fear of the Lord is the beginning of knowledge"* (Proverbs 1:7a).

THE WICKED'S FINAL DESTINY

What knowledge did the Psalmist get from God's sanctuary? *The first lesson he received was that the wicked have a final destiny.* Notice the action and result clause in verse 17. The action is he entered the sanctuary of God. The result comes at the end of the verse. It says, *"then I understood their final destiny."* You don't receive understanding until you enter God's house for worship and study. When he came into God's presence, he received the perspective he needed to deal with the confusing questions that troubled him in the world.

What did he learn about the wicked's destiny? *First, he learned that their destiny was certain.* He writes in verse 18, *"Surely you place them on slippery ground; you cast them down to ruin."* The emphasis in this verse is upon the word *surely*. It's a word of confidence, conviction and complete certainty. The wicked will not remain in control. Their doom is certain. They will bow to God's sovereignty one day. Truth will prevail. Right will conquer wrong. It is certain. It is from God. Count on it.

The story is told of a farmer in a small Midwestern town that had a strong hatred for the church next door to his property. He would deliberately plow his fields beside the church's sanctuary so that he could distract the membership during morning worship. When church members would arrive for the early service, he would shake his fist at them as they walked up the sidewalk.

When October came, this farmer had his finest crop ever. In fact, county records showed that it was the best in the area. When his harvest was complete, he placed an ad in the local newspaper that bashed Christians for their faith in God. Near the end of the article he stated, "Having faith in God doesn't mean much if He prospers me like this!"

Because this was a small town, the paper asked the pastor of the local church to respond to this article. In a calm and polite manner, the next edition off the press contained a small ad that simply stated, "To our farmer-friend: God doesn't always settle His accounts in October." This answer parallels the lesson learned by the Psalmist. Things may look smooth and good right now for the wicked. But their end is sure.

The second thing he learned about the wicked's destiny is that it is sudden. Verse 19 reveals their future, *"How suddenly are they destroyed, completely swept away by terrors! As a dream when one awakes, so when you arise, O Lord, you will despise them as fantasies."* The Psalmist realized that the wicked occupy the spotlight for a short time. In God's time, when He is finished with them, they will be removed quickly. They are here today, gone tomorrow.

Father Henry Fehren wrote a good article in *Christianity Today*[1] about the sudden destiny of the wicked. He wrote that the evil person is like the man that jumped from the 50th floor of an office building without a parachute. When he passed the 30th floor on his way down, someone looked out and shouted, "How's it going? The jumper answered, "So far so good." This story pictures a clear truth. It's only a matter of time before the wicked receive their fate. In fact, they're plunging to their doom right now. You may not see it always, but they're going to it quicker than you think. The destiny of the wicked summarizes the first lesson the Psalmist learned in God's sanctuary.

GOD'S LIFE RESOURCES DURING TIMES OF CONFUSION

The second lesson the Psalmist received in the sanctuary is the life resources God offers us during times of confusion. Beginning with verse 23, Asaph states at least five important things that he received from God when He sought Him during times of confusion. When things don't make sense, these assets are available when you make God the priority in your life.

The first resource he received was God's presence. Even when he was grieved and embittered at his state of affairs, he writes in verse 23, *"Yet I am always with you; you hold me by my right hand."* When he entered God's sanctuary, he came face to face with his Maker and Lord. This awareness of God's presence helped him to realize that he wasn't alone. Someone was there, ready to help him in his time of need. Likewise for us, the lesson is clear. When you're confused, go to God's house and seek His presence. You will leave with a greater understanding of God than you had when you first came.

---

[1] *Christianity Today* (Volume 30, number 12).

In his exposition of Psalm 73, D. Martyn Lloyd-Jones wrote, "The house of God has delivered me from 'the mumps and measles of the soul a thousand times and more—merely to enter its doors.'"[2] What enabled him to say that? From experience, he knew that when he stood with God's people in the Lord's presence for worship, the affairs of this world were put into perspective. Likewise, the Psalmist learned the mind of God from times of worship in His sanctuary. You and I can learn that lesson, too.

The second resource he received was God's guidance. In verse 24, the Psalmist writes, *"You guide me with your counsel, and afterward you will take me into glory."* Not only did Asaph receive God's perspective to understand the situation he faced, but also he received wisdom to help him *handle* the matter on a day-to-day basis. God guided him with insight for daily living as he encountered the wicked on a regular basis. This brings home an important point. Many times God doesn't give the total answer to the complete problem from one sitting. He gives us what we need *today* so that we can handle it with His empowerment, then come back to Him for more.

I once heard Corrie Ten Boom tell a story in a radio interview that speaks to the heart of this issue. She stated that as she came home from church one evening, she was struggling to recognize God's guidance for her life. Suddenly, she drove into a dense fog and could see nothing. Poking her head out the window, she noticed a tiny light from the road ahead. As her car slowly moved forward, those small lights blinked out. Another set of oncoming headlights took its place a few yards later. She crawled along, following the short distance she could see, one light after another, until the fog cleared. Then it hit her. She realized that this is how God guided her. He showed her how far she needed to go at any given moment. And step-by-step, she moved from one light to the next. Confident of God's guidance, she let go of the need to see His complete plan all at once. This approach probably paralleled the Psalmist as well. He received God's daily guidance when he regularly entered His sanctuary.

The third resource he received in God's sanctuary was His contentment. Realizing that His Heavenly Father was intimately acquainted with all his ways and knowing His nearness to help in

---

[2] D. Martyn Lloyd-Jones, *Faith on Trial* (Baker, 1965), p. 39.

times of confusion, the Psalmist writes in verse 25, *"Whom have I in heaven but you? And being with you, I desire nothing on earth."* Like David, he experienced the validity of Psalm 16:11, *"You have made known to me the path of life; you will fill me with joy in your presence, with eternal pleasures at your right hand."* When Asaph entered the sanctuary, God's intimate relationship satisfied his heart and gave him the consolation needed to accept the confusing things he witnessed in the world. Despite the disturbing events around him, He knew his Heavenly Father gave assurance to know that *"in all things God works for the good of those who love him, who have been called according to his purpose"* (Romans 8:28).

When I think about assurance, I'm reminded of the life of Fanny Crosby (1820-1915), the famous American hymn writer. When she was only six weeks old, she was blinded through an improper medical treatment upon her eyes. Yet as she matured, she never considered blindness a handicap, but rather a blessing in her life. At the tender age of eight, she wrote these words that characterized her view of life:

> O what a happy soul am I!
> Although I cannot see,
> I am resolved that in this world
> Contented I will be;
> How many blessings I enjoy
> That other people don't.
> To weep and sigh because I'm blind,
> I cannot, and I won't.[3]

It was this strong presence of divine contentment that marked her life. One time later in adult life a Scottish minister said to her in passing, "I think it is a great pity that the Master, when He showered so many gifts upon you, did not give you sight." She replied, "Do you know that if at birth I had been able to make one petition to my Creator, it would have been that I should be born blind?" The surprised clergyman asked, "Why?" Miss Crosby's response is classic: "Because when I get to heaven, the first face that shall ever gladden my sight will be that of my Savior." Like the Psalmist, the

---

[3] Fanny Crosby, *An Autobiography*. Grand Rapids: Baker Book House, 1986.

Apostle Paul (Philippians 4: 11) and many others through history, she learned to trust God when times of confusion came. This gave her great contentment to face each day with renewed peace.

The fourth resource the Psalmist received in God's sanctuary was His strength. He writes in verse 26, *"My flesh and my heart may fail, but God is the strength of my heart and my portion forever."* While trouble and confusion abounded on the outside, the writer felt peace and harmony on the inside because the power of God filled his life, enabling him to draw courage to face the world around him. Like another Psalmist, he knew that *"God is our refuge and strength, an ever present help in trouble"* (Psalm 46:1). There was a power from within that enabled him to manage and to control the pressures of life that came from watching the activity of the wicked.

Jay Kesler wrote a story in *Leadership* Magazine several years ago that hits this point on the bull's eye. He was writing about the two ways people handled pressure. One way was pictured by a bathysphere, a miniature submarine used to explore the ocean in places so deep that the water pressure would crush a conventional submarine easily. Bathyspheres were constructed with plates of steel several inches thick in certain places. This kept water out, but it also made it heavy and difficult to maneuver. The people on the inside were cramped.

However, when these vessels descend to the ocean floor, they find they're not alone. When their lights are turned on and the people look through the tiny, thick plate glass windows, what do they see? Fish! How do these fish survive this kind of pressure? Kesler's point hits the target. These fish deal with extreme pressure in an entirely different way. They don't build thick skins on the outside. Instead, they remain supple and free. They compensate for the outside pressure through *equal and opposite pressure inside* themselves. Likewise, Christians don't have to be hard and thick skinned as long as they appropriate God's power within to equal the pressure without. Where do they find God's power and strength to handle the pressure? They do what the Psalmist did. They go to God directly! They receive His strength when they go to His sanctuary.

The fifth resource the Psalmist received from God's sanctuary was His protection. He states this in verse 28, *"But as for me, it is good to be near God. I have made the Sovereign Lord my refuge; I will tell of all your deeds."* In times of storm, the Lord was his shelter and defense. When he acknowledged his need, God came to fight the battles for him. Under His wings, he could rest in the safety of His care.

When I think of divine protection from the evil one, I'm reminded of an event in the life of David Brainerd, the famous missionary to the North American Indians that illustrates this truth. When he first came among the Indians, he was not received. In fact, some tried to kill him soon after he arrived. One day as they crept toward his tent, they cautiously peered under the flap. They saw Brainerd praying on his knees. As he prayed, a rattlesnake entered the tent and came close to his feet. No one knows for sure if the Indians placed the snake in the tent or if it entered on it's own. In either case, the natives' intention to kill him faded as they watched the movement of the snake. As it moved into a coiled position to strike, all of a sudden it lowered its head and glided out of the tent. From that moment on, the Indians held Brainerd in high honor among the village. They looked upon him as a messenger from the Great Spirit, protected by Him in times of danger and peril. He went on to establish a significant ministry that witnessed hundreds of Native Americans won to the Lord Jesus and many others led into full-time missionary service. His life was kept in the shadow of His Savior's protection.

Divine protection, along with strength, guidance, contentment and the presence of God are available to those who seek God's presence when times of confusion come into their life. They worked for Asaph in this psalm and they can work for you today. The issue to address is, "will I come into God's presence and claim them?"

SUMMARY

Psalm 73 provides some insight into the question, "Where is God when things don't make sense to me?" It reminds us that we can't see everything clearly from our perspective. This confusion should drive us to God to see what lessons we can learn about His character and His plan for us in our time of need. When we come into His presence, we should not only ask Him, "Why?" but also "What?"— "God, what do you want me to learn and to experience about your presence, guidance, contentment, strength and protection?" When we seek the face of Jesus, He will give us the perspective and the resources needed to handle the issues that trouble us in the world.

APPLICATION

Are you struggling with confusion today? Are you wrestling with issues that don't make sense right now? God has you where He wants you! Begin by confessing to Him that you need help to see things from *HIS* perspective, not yours. In addition to this, remember that the struggles you face today are intended to help you learn more about Christ and His available grace. Remember, our Lord faced hardships and questions when He lived upon the earth. Yet in a wonderful way, the Scriptures tell us that "He learned obedience from what He suffered" (Hebrews 5:8). Cheer up! God wants you to grow during this time of confusion in your life! Be encouraged! The fight will not be forever!

PRAYER

Heavenly Father, forgive me for the times that I have looked upon things from my own perspective instead of Yours. In so many ways, I have failed to seek Your presence in Your House in order to understand the things that confuse me. Today I want to start afresh with You again. I intentionally commit myself into Your care, asking that You give me Your strength, presence, contentment and guidance as I rest under the wings of Your protection. I know You want me to learn some great things about Yourself and about me in this whole process. I humbly ask today for the mind of Christ. Make this day a new beginning for me in Your sight. Through Christ My Savior, in whose Name I pray. AMEN.

TALK TIME!

1. What is confusing you today? What doesn't make sense in your life? In the world around you? What makes these things so oppressive?
2. How do you handle the questions that don't have a clear answer?

Look up Proverbs 25:2, Isaiah 45:15, Deuteronomy 29:29a and Ecclesiastes 11:5. What does this say? Does this give you insight to God's view of your life situations?

3. What do you think about God when all this is going on? How do you relate to Him?

4. What lessons strike you as you study Psalm 73? Is there comfort in knowing that the wicked's destiny is final, certain and sudden? How does this comfort you?

5. Review the resources mentioned by the Psalmist, starting at verse 23 that are available when you seek God's presence. Which one especially do you need today?

6. "From God's point of view, what we need to learn from those moments is not only to ask Him, *"WHY?"* but also *"WHAT?"* Is this difficult to do? Why or why not?

7. Do you know someone who is struggling today with these issues too? How can this lesson equip you to help them?

2

WHEN TIMES OF DISCOURAGEMENT COME

"Why are you downcast, O my soul?
Why so disturbed within me?
Psalm 42:5a

It may have happened a long time ago in my first year of ministry when I was in my mid-twenties, but the embers still spark within me whenever I think about it. Just eight months into my internship in church planting, I was face to face with a major confrontation. The three families that called me to start this new church in Oklahoma asked for a meeting with the presbytery's oversight committee, my wife and me. As I look back at that meeting, I know that my immaturity blindsided me and I didn't see things ahead of time. The writing was all over the wall. I was a calf headed for the butcher.

After an opening prayer, the chairman of the committee looked around and said, "We're here today to review the progress on the work up to this point and to offer any constructive input to help us in this ministry. Who wants to be first?" After a brief pause, the head layman of the group began to list the things that had been done in the past eight months, noting every time the numbers, the cost and the effectiveness of each item. He was used to this method from his many management years in business. As an aggressive executive looking for something to do in his retirement, it appeared this ministry had become his pet project. So he poured his time and attention into it. He was well into his sixty's and I was in my mid-twenties. He wanted to lead. In my opinion, I was there for the ride. I think you get the picture.

As we listened to his report, I could tell in the tone of his voice that something was not right. Where I was positioned in the room, I could see his wife over his shoulder. The more he talked, the more intense she became. Finally like a volcano, she erupted in the room, saying all kinds of things about me in the presence of the other families. I sunk lower into my chair with every passing comment.

"It's not working with him," she said. "He's not the kind of pastor that we need for us and for this small town. We need someone with more mature people skills that can go out and touch people and bring them in. He needs to find another place to serve." With these and other remarks, I found myself sliding to the bottom of the chair, stunned with bewilderment. "Are you okay?" a person asked. "Sure," I said, trying to sit up and to disguise the pain and dejection. "This was a good meeting. I'm glad people expressed their opinions. I'll grow from this, I'm sure."

I received a pill of discouragement that day that I know the doctor didn't order. But it was served on a silver platter and I still feel the effects of it many years later. The things said at that meeting plunged into my heart like an emotional knife. It's not just what they said. It's *how they said it.* They didn't stop with an initial stab. Their repetitious phrases turned that knife several times in my system to make a lifelong memory. I walked away a dejected young pastor wondering why God called me to do this. At that stage of my life, I couldn't remember a time of greater discouragement.

Ever had one of those times? Over the years, many people have told me their discouraging experiences. For some, it came from their spouse and their actions. Others have watched their children go down the wrong path. I've also seen people blown away from a decline in their business and left wondering if they can rebound. Another person comes to my mind right now that was turned down for a job promotion and pay raise. He took a stand on a moral issue with which the company disagreed, bringing opposition from upper management. You don't have to live long to experience discouragement. Every human being faces it often in their life.

I like the words the English novelist James Payn wrote in describing the effect of discouragement brings to our life:

> I never had a piece of toast
> Particularly long and wide

But fell upon the sanded floor,
And always on the buttered side.[4]

Discouragement comes when the buttered side of your life lands on the dirty floor. When this happens, have you ever said, "God, Where are You?" When times of deep disappointment come, have you wondered where God is when you really need Him? Does He have some words of comfort for me if I come to Him? Does He really care enough to help?

Throughout the Bible, you see many people that struggled with heartache and the pain of disappointment. Abraham, Moses, Joshua, Elijah, David and many of the Prophets encountered times of personal sorrow and despair over a number of things. Sometimes their discouragement came from their lot in life. They were entrusted with difficult things to do and at times they didn't see any progress. Sometimes it was other people that opposed them in the work, bringing added turmoil and grief. Many times they became depressed over the spiritual decay in their own life. I'm sure they felt like many of us today as we look at our own spiritual condition before God. I know I've looked at the sin in my own life many times and have become discouraged about it. I've asked God at times, "If I'm supposed to be the leader and I look this bad on the inside, why export it?" Ever felt that way?

There is good news in this journey! God has some important lessons for us in our times of deep disappointment. In Psalm 42, God wants to show us some important things about Himself, our own inner lives and our need to turn to Him. You can discover some answers to help you deal with disappointment and to empower you to overcome it in your daily life.

LESSON FOCUS

When times of discouragement come into your life, seek God's face through worship and prayer, relying on His hope and love to get you through it. God can be trusted when you hit the down times in your life because He has experienced it in the person of Jesus, His Son.

---

[4] James Payn, *Chambers Journal* (February 2, 1884).

It's a Regular Occurrence

Twice in Psalm 42, the question is raised, *"Why are you down-cast, O my soul? Why so disturbed within me?"* (v. 5,11). The psalmist spends significant self-reflection on his state of life. His soul is burdened and his conscience is low. The fact that he asks this question twice indicates two things about him. First, it tells me that discouragement dominated his mind. The emotion of the question is moving. He asks himself, "why am I so down? Why am I so distraught?" The emphasis is on "why." It was a question that consumed his thinking.

The second thing it tells me about him is that his discouragement was regular. There must have been several things happening in his life that pulled his spirit into emotional mud. These things nagged him. They were like "shoo flies" that wouldn't go away. They pestered him and pulled him down into a quagmire of personal doubt. Because of this, he didn't feel good about himself or about life in general.

Sources of Discouragement

What was bothering the psalmist in his day? As you read the text, you see that *his first source of discouragement was oppression.* In verse 9 we read, *"I say to God my Rock, 'Why have you forgotten me? Why must I go about mourning, oppressed by the enemy?"* Discouragement came when he saw his enemies mock the Great Name of God, taunting His actions and defying His Sovereign rule. Most of them wanted nothing to do with God or God's work.

Although many centuries separate his day from our day, this picture is still an accurate one for our time. You see so many things today that mock Name of Christ in the public eye. Modern depictions of art that ridicule the sacrificial death of Christ on the Cross are housed in taxpayer-supported museums. Legislation continues to surface supporting the gay and lesbian agendas of homosexual activists. The U.S. Supreme Court continues to attack the rightful place of student-led prayer in the public school system. In addition to this, famous phrases such as "In God We Trust" and "One Nation under God" that are engraved into our public buildings and our treasury coinage are consistently threatened for removal. Like the psalmist in his day, we face serious opposition in our time.

Sometimes we look at the opposition's activity and we get discouraged. We take a stand on many of these issues and the world responds with various attacks. Sometimes it's physical. But for the most part, at least for now, it's verbal. I'm sure this will change as time marches on. The intensity is bound to increase. The Psalmist experienced attacks *"all day long"* (v. 10). Likewise, many believers are under the continuous barrage of attack from enemy oppressors today. And many times this brings discouragement.

You may be surprised at the second source of his discouragement. *It was God.* In the Psalmist's mind, God was considerably absent from his life. In verse 9, he asks the Lord, *"Why have you forgotten me?"* Notice how his enemies take advantage of this situation by saying twice in the text, *"Where is your God?"* (v. 3,9). This fueled his discouragement because God didn't intervene at a time when he needed deliverance and power. From his perspective, God was far away. He asked for help, but didn't get it.

Felt that way lately? I'm sure you have. Too many times, we've asked God to intervene in a situation or in a person. And nothing happens. We go to Him and say, "Why? Why didn't you do something? You had the perfect opportunity! But you let it slip away. Why?"

To muddy the water more, you hear nothing back from Him. There is silence from above. You sense God is a great distance away, unwilling to do anything to help you. And the more you ponder it, the more discouraged you feel. You probably felt like throwing in the towel and giving up. I'm sure the Psalmist felt that way at times. Yet in the midst of his times of sorrow, he learned some valuable principles about God and about God's plan for overcoming discouragement by turning it into a growing experience.

DISCOURAGEMENT CAN MAKE YOU THIRST FOR GOD

The first principle the Psalmist experienced in the down times of his life was that *the dryness of his soul made him thirst for the presence of God.* Verses 1-2 state, *"As the deer pants for streams of water, so my soul pants for you, O God. My soul thirsts for God, for*

21

the living God. When can I go and meet God?" In his times of discouragement, he realized a choice existed in his life. Either he would go away from God, reject His face and live with a hardened heart or he would turn to God, seek His face and live with a thirsty soul. As we can see from the text, he turned to the Lord. He thirsted for God's presence. He sought His face. He knew the Lord was the only true source of help for His life. And when he turned, he discovered two important lessons in his spiritual walk.

The first lesson he experienced during discouragement was that worship becomes real when you turn to the Lord. While people oppressed him and drove him to tears with their jests, the Psalmist said in verse 4, *"These things I remember as I pour out my soul: how I used to go with the multitude, leading the procession to the house of God, with shouts of joy and thanksgiving among the festive throng."* He remembered those times in his life when he would go with the people of God into the House of God. They were times of great celebration and unparalleled thanksgiving. And in his time of dismay, he longed for it with all his heart.

Good worship will help you get through times of great discouragement. Yet I find many Christians doing just the opposite in their practice. They stay away from the House of God. They wallow in their misery, choosing to baste in their own self-pity instead of coming to the Throne of Grace for help in their time of need. I plead with you to understand this. *When you are discouraged, you need more than ever to worship Almighty God.* In worship, you draw strength from the Lord and you gain encouragement from fellow believers to persevere with courage. The next time you face a time where you're down in the dumps, don't miss a worship service.

The second lesson the Psalmist experienced during discouragement was the reality of prayer. He writes in verse 6, *"My soul is downcast within me; therefore I will remember you from the land of the Jordan, the heights of Hermon—from Mount Mizar."* In verse 8, he states, *"By day the Lord directs His love, at night His song is with me—a prayer to the God of my life."* The Psalmist understood the same principle with prayer as he did with worship. When you become discouraged, you can either turn to the Lord in prayer or you can turn away from Him. It's only in turning the Lord that we find comfort.

This lesson underscores the absolute importance of a quiet time. Time spent alone each day with God is vital to keep your perspective on track and your attitude in check. At this point, I'm *not* going to advise you *when* you need to have your quiet time or *how* you have one. I find those issues are answered when you decide that you *will* have some time alone with God. A time of Bible reading and conversation with God keeps you focused on the big picture. It helps you see your need for God and for His grace and courage in times of trial and loneliness. You can experience tremendous growth in times of discouragement when you spend some time alone with God.

Times of discouragement can make your spiritual life bear fruit in the sight of God. The Psalmist used those disappointing times to turn him to God. When he thirsted for God and remembered His love, he received grace in the down moments of his life. In a similar way, some of your greatest opportunities for growth will come when you sense a spirit of hopelessness within you. It's important to keep everything in perspective. Things don't grow on top of a mountain. They blossom in the valley.

WHAT TO DO IN TIMES OF DISCOURAGEMENT

Most of us have been on the receiving end of broken promises, unfair actions and derogatory accusations that have little merit. When they come, they hurt and bring discouragement. It's at this point that we have a choice to make. Either we sit in mental misery or we choose to grow from it. From the Psalmist's example, we can learn some things that can help us get through these times of pressure and emotional hardship. The next time you face a situation that seeks to pull you down through discouragement, follow these action steps.

The first action step is to put your hope in the Lord. In verse 5 and 11 he writes, *"Why are you downcast, O my soul? Why so disturbed within me?"* Notice his immediate response: *"Put your hope in God."* This hope that he refers to is not wishful thinking or mindless optimism. It's also not a blind leap into the dark. It's a fixed trust in the Lord and a belief that says, *"My times are in your hands"* (Psalm 31:15a). It's a deliberate commitment you make to put your life into God's care and to draw from Him the hope you need during your wilderness times. It's active, not passive.

Charles Haddon Spurgeon, one of the greatest preachers of the 19th century, once preached these comforting words about trust and hope: "So then, poor Christian, thou needest not go pumping up thy poor heart to make it glad. Go to thy Maker, and ask Him to give thee a song in the night. Thou art a poor dry well: thou hast heard it said, that when a pump is dry, you must pour water down it first of all, and then you will get some up; and so, Christian, when thou art dry, go to God, ask Him to pour some joy down thee, and then thou wilt get some joy up from thine heart."[5] This kind of sight comes only to those who look up, not in.

What does it really mean to look up? Recently I read this story by Jeanette Strong that illustrates this truth in a simple and practical way:

> When my son was a toddler, washing his hair was always a problem. He would sit in the bathtub while I put shampoo on his hair. Then, when I poured on the water to make a lather, he would tip his head down so that the shampoo ran into his eyes, causing pain and tears. I explained that if he just looked straight up at me, he could avoid getting the shampoo in his face. He would agree; then, as soon as I started to rinse his hair, his fear would overcome his trust, and he would look down again. Naturally the shampoo would run into his face again, and there would be more tears. During one of our sessions, while I was trying to convince him to lift up his head and trust me, I suddenly realized how this situation was like my relationship to God. I know God is my Father, and I'm sure He loves me. I believe that I trust Him, but sometimes, in a difficult situation, I panic and turn my eyes away from Him. This never solves the problem; I just become more afraid, as the "shampoo" blinds me.
>
> Even though my son knew I loved him, he had a hard

---

[5] Charles Spurgeon, "Songs in the Night" in *The Protestant Pulpit* (Abingdon-Cokesbury Press, 1947), p. 114-128.

time trusting me in a panicky situation. I knew I could protect him, but convincing him of that wasn't easy, especially when all he could see was water coming down. His lack of trust hurt me, but it hurt him more. He was the one who had to suffer the pain. I'm sure my lack of trust hurts God very much, but how much more does it hurt me?

Often in the Bible, we are told to lift up our head to God when problems come. He knows how to protect us if we remember to listen to Him. Now, when I find myself in a situation where it would be easy to panic, I picture my son sitting in the bathtub, looking up at me, learning to trust me. Then I ask God what I should do. Sometimes the answer may seem scary, but one thing I'm sure of— He'll never pour shampoo in my face![6]

The second action step in a time of discouragement is to remember the Lord's love and presence. Notice the action verb "remember" in verse 6, *"My soul is downcast within me; therefore I will remember you…"* When times of heartache and inner trouble come, remember God's promise to be near you. He has said in His Word, *"He will never leave you nor forsake you"* (Deuteronomy 31:6b). The action step is to engage this thought with initiative and boldness by saying at the start of each day, "I know God is with me and His love and presence will make a difference in my life today." Count on God to come through for you! Trust Him with your down times! Give Him your worries! Depend on His presence to help you! He wants to be near *YOU*! Remember it!

Oswald Chambers wrote these inspiring words about the help God offers us:

He will take you up, He will re-make you, He will make your soul young and will restore to you the years that the cankerworm hath eaten, and place you higher than the loftiest mountain peak, safe in the arms of the Lord Himself, secure from all alarms, and with an imper-

---

[6] Original story found in James S. Hewett, *Illustrations Unlimited* (Wheaton: Tyndale House Publishers, Inc, 1988), p. 479.

turbable peace that the world cannot take away...Oh, the security, the ineffable rest of knowing that the God who made the mountains can come to our help![7]

God wants to love us today with grace beyond measure. The question remains, "Will I ask Him for it?"

The third action step in a time of discouragement is to worship God. Feel the passion in the Psalmist's heart as he writes in verse 2, *"My soul thirsts for God, for the living God. When can I go and meet with God?"* Remember the Lord's House and come with a thirsty heart. The lasting answers to the life problems you face will not come from a do-it-yourself book or an expensive seminar on stress management. They will come when you fix your heart upon the beauty and holiness of Almighty God in worship. Personal and corporate exaltation will lead you out of the valley onto the mountaintops with God.

One of the best definitions of worship I have ever seen comes from the mind of Archbishop William Temple (1881-1944) who wrote, "To worship is to quicken the conscience by the holiness of God, to feed the mind with the truth of God, to purge the imagination by the beauty of God, to open the heart to the love of God and to devote the will to the purpose of God."[8] What more can be said! Worship, like hope and remembering, is active. All three call us to engage our mind and soul in positive ways. They form a positive action plan under God's power to move us out of discouragement into levelheaded living.

SUMMARY AND APPLICATION

We face regular times of discouragement in our lives from many sources. They should motivate us to look up to God for help and for answers instead of looking within ourselves. It's only when we place our trust in Him, remembering His love and presence and worshiping Him in spirit and truth that we gain the strength and perspective to look at the disappointing times with meaning and pur-

---

[7] Oswald Chambers, *The Place of Help* (London: Simpkin Marshall, LTD., 1935), p. 5,6.
[8] William Temple, *Readings in St. John's Gospel, First Series* (London: Macmillan and Company, 1940), p. 68.

pose. God wants you to look up. Will you?

Your Stains Can Be Gains

Over a hundred years ago in a Scottish seaside inn, a group of fishermen were relaxing after a long day at sea. As a waitress walked past the fishermen's table with a pot of tea, one of the men made a sweeping gesture with his hand as he told a tall fisherman's tale. When he did, it collided with the tray and sent the teapot crashing against the whitewashed wall, leaving several large brown stains.

Standing nearby, the innkeeper surveyed the damage. He said, "that stain will never come out. The whole wall will have to be painted." Then a voice from the other side of the room sounded, "Perhaps not." All eyes turned to look at this stranger. The innkeeper said to him, "What do you mean?" The outsider said, "Let me work with this stain. If my work meets your approval, you will not need to paint the wall." The innkeeper agreed.

The stranger picked up his metal box and approached the wall. Out of it came pencils, brushes and some glass jars full of linseed oil and pigment. He began to sketch lines around the stain, filling in places with color and shading. Soon, a picture emerged. Those tea stains turned into a magnificent buck with a beautiful rack of antlers.

Then, at the bottom of the picture, the man inscribed his signature. He paid for his meal, then left the inn. When everyone gathered around the picture, they saw that the signature read, "E.H. Landseer." They received a visit from world-renowned wildlife artist Sir Edwin Landseer. He took several stains on a wall and made something beautiful out of it.

What stains are in your life today? What is discouraging you? God wants to paint a beautiful portrait in your life, using those disappointments. He wants to show you Himself in a great way. Will you let Him?

Prayer

Heavenly Father, as I look around today, I see things that bring discouragement and disappointment in my life. I get down when other people fail me. I lose heart when circumstances go against me. I also sink when I look at my own sin and personal shortcomings. Dear Lord, in the midst of my low moments, help me to put my hope and trust in You. Remind me of your great love and never failing presence that is with me wherever I go. Give me a heart that longs to worship you with sincerity and passion. Today I hunger and thirst for Your presence and grace in my life. I want the Mind of Christ in everything I do. Grant this request I pray. In the powerful Name of Christ I ask, AMEN.

TALK TIME!

1. What are the things that bring discouragement to your life? When you get discouraged, how do you respond?
2. "Things don't grow on top of a mountain. They blossom in the valley." Discuss.
3. Review the three things to do when disappointment comes in your life. Which one is the easiest to do? Which one is the toughest to do?
4. Review the closing story about E.H. Landseer. What can you learn from it?
5. Do you know someone that is discouraged today? How can this lesson equip you to help that person?

3

FAILURE IS NOT FINAL

"Then Peter remembered the word Jesus had spoken, 'Before the rooster crows, you will disown me three times.' And he went outside and wept bitterly."
Matthew 26:75

My wife surprised me a few days ago when she checked out a book tape from the county public library on Winston Churchill. She normally doesn't read books, but with her daily travels from school to school as a physical therapist, she decided to listen to something worthwhile. So I listened to the cassettes when I drove her car. The series recalls many significant events in the life of the famed British leader. One episode stood out in my mind.

One time a reporter asked Churchill, "What prepared you the most to lead Great Britain through World War II?" Powerful question! You'll recall that during this time in history, England was the only country that defied the claims of Hitler and Mussolini. It took great courage for a person to speak into the darkness alone. What enabled Churchill to do it? Here was his response: "It was the time I repeated a class in grade school." The reporter appeared stunned and countered, "You mean you flunked a grade?" Churchill replied, "I *never* flunked in my life. I was given a second opportunity to get it right."

What an attitude! That's the secret to victory in times of apparent defeat. Think about John James Audubon. From 1808 to 1820, he lived mostly in Kentucky going from one job to another, never resting upon an occupation that fulfilled him. He lived as a drifter. One could conclude that his early adult life showed no signs of direction. However, from 1823 to 1828, he converted his time and passion to a full-time career in bird observation and painting, teaching drawing in New Orleans and West Feliciana parish,

Louisiana. There he perfected his efforts in painting, securing a British publisher for his bird drawings in 1826. The rest is history. His portraits remain one of the great achievements in environmental art over the last two centuries. What started as a ho-hum life turned into a great accomplishment. For him, it all centered on perspective, finding something that produces passion in him and pursuing it with all his heart.

Perhaps the most powerful lesson on failure comes from the life of Abraham Lincoln. When he was seven, his family was driven out of their home, forcing him to work at an early age. When he reached nine, his mother died. He lost his job as a store clerk at age twenty-two. The next year, he went into major debt to become a partner in a small store. However, tragedy struck when his business partner died three years later, leaving him an enormous balance that took him years to repay. At age twenty-eight, after courting a girl for four years, she said NO to his marriage proposal. It took him three times to get elected to Congress, only to experience failure two years later when he sought reelection. At age forty-one, his heart broke when his four-year-old son died. He lost in the 1855 Senate race and was defeated the next year as a vice-presidential candidate. When he reached forty-nine, he ran for the Senate again, but lost. By any observation, most people would see his life as a trail of tears. But look what happened in 1860! He was elected the sixteenth President of the United States at age fifty-one. To this day, most historians regard "honest Abe" as one of the finest leaders America has ever known. His secret? A correct response to failure and defeat.

Failure is not something people want to discuss much less experience in the real world. From the football player who watches the other team kick the game winning field goal with no time remaining on the clock to the student who tries but cannot make a passing grade on a final exam, failure bites everyone, young and old.

Over the years, all of us can think of everyday people who suffered defeats. Remember the respected parents in the PTA who reared normal children, only to see them turn rebellious in the teenage years? Son or daughter grew up and followed the wrong crowd into a life of moral defeats and troubles that stayed with them for the rest of their lives. Remember the couple that tried to start a family, but repeatedly ran into fertility difficulties?

Perhaps you know of a person who was given a pink slip at work and told to come back to the unemployment line next week. I'm sure all of us can picture the faces of people who have suffered through marital collapse and divorce. Failure can touch the little child who was inadvertently left off the birthday invitation list all the way to the corporate investor who lost millions of dollars in a Stock Market plunge. I've seen it broadside single parents who cannot make ends meet. Their car is broken down. They have no emergency savings account and the college tuition bill is sitting on the kitchen table. They know they cannot pay it, yet they work sixty hours a week.

Let me get personal. *You have experienced failure in your personal life.* Perhaps it's not from one of the above examples, but you remember the times when you felt ruined. Those experiences hurt. They pierced your insides and continue to bring pain into your life when you think about it. Because of these past events, you may be thinking that the label "FAILURE" is stuck to your forehead.

I want to challenge that assumption from Scripture, using the examples of two important people. By studying Matthew 26 and 27, we can learn these important principles from the lives of Judas and Peter:

- Yes, both failed miserably. Peter denied the Lord. Judas betrayed Him.
- God used that experience to bring them to a crossroads in their lives where they had a decision to make—either turn to Him in repentance and receive restoration or turn away from Him and live in hopelessness.

The choice was their's to make. It's also a choice before us.

LESSON FOCUS

From the example of Judas and Peter, we learn that the world views failure as a door to a hopeless end. However from God's perspective, we can experience failure as a door to an endless hope. It all depends on your willingness to accept, to learn and to grow from your setbacks.

31

FAILURE BITES EVERYONE

When you study the Passion of Christ, you can feel the pain when Judas and Peter realized their failure before the Lord. In Peter's life, it comes in Matthew 26:75, *"Then Peter remembered the word Jesus had spoken: 'Before the rooster crows, you will disown me three times."* In Judas' life, it comes in Matthew 27:3, *"When Judas, who had betrayed him, saw that Jesus was condemned, he was seized with remorse and returned the thirty silver coins to the chief priests and the elders. 'I have sinned,' he said, 'for I have betrayed innocent blood."* Both of these men knew what they did was wrong. On the one hand, Peter denied knowing Jesus Christ, the Son of God. On the other hand, Judas wanted everyone to know his relationship to the Messiah so that he could sell Him to the authorities for money. Peter *denied*. Judas *betrayed*. Both made critical, life-changing mistakes and they paid dearly for them.

What failures did these men commit? *From both of their actions, you first see failure in loyalty.* Peter denied Christ. Another way to say it is *he disowned Him*. This is seen in 26:72, *"He denied it again, with an oath: 'I don't know the man!'"* This phrase "the man" can mean "this fellow," a term used to denote the common man on the street. It carries no honor or respect at all. In other words, Peter labeled Christ before other people. By making this statement, he disowned his relationship to Christ. He turned away from Him, despite the fact that ten chapters earlier, he voiced with passion, *"You are the Christ, the Son of the living God"* (Matthew 16:16). He failed to be a loyal friend.

Likewise, Judas was one of the twelve disciples of Christ, picked by Jesus Himself to accompany Him in ministry. He saw the Lord of Glory teach, heal, confront, restore and bring encouragement to the downcast. He was an eyewitness of His amazing work. Yet he betrayed Him for money. He failed to be a loyal follower.

Ever felt the sting of disloyalty? Maybe you told a secret to a friend in confidence and he leaked it. Perhaps it was when a person made a promise to help you with something and didn't follow through. I know from my own experience that if I could collect every year on the times someone broke a promise to me, I'd make a sizable annual contribution toward my IRA. To a degree, imagine how Jesus felt when the people closest to Him became traitors in their relationship. It not only hurts. *It hurts deeply for a long time. Second, from both of their actions, you see failure in witness.* In Peter's life, when several sensed that his accent identified him as one of Jesus' disciples, it says in Matthew 26:74, *"Then he began to call down curses on himself and he swore to them, 'I don't know the man!'"* Clearly, Peter lied. As a disciple, he was not only a learner, but also a follower. Instead of speaking up for Christ at an opportune time, he chose to deny any association with Him. He had the perfect occasion to voice a word for His Lord when Christ needed him the most. Instead, he chose to deny and to retreat.

Judas' actions reveal the same failure in witness. In Matthew 26:48 we read, *"Now the betrayer had arranged a signal with them: 'The one I kiss is the man; arrest him.'"* Instead of pointing people to Christ as the Savior of the world, Judas used the Lord for personal gain. He made Christ the source of town division instead of hope. Like Peter, he had a golden opportunity to witness for the Lord before the religious leaders of the day. He could set the record straight. But he chose to sell rather than speak.

If we took an honest inventory of ourselves, we would see similar failures and defeats in our lives. We fail others in our relationships, our trust, our witness and our commitments. Like Babe Ruth, we strike out often (in his case it was 1,330 times). We want to be dependable hitters, but when the moment of opportunity arrives, many times we watch the third strike. When this happens, a price is paid. For some people, their defeats turn into instant collapse. For others, it's long-term misery. In both situations, the consequences are long-lived and significant.

IS THERE HOPE?

Over the years, I've talked to many people who have experienced some kind of failure in their lives. One who comes to my mind at this point is a guy I'll call "Stan." He experienced great success as a real estate broker, amassing tremendous income from business properties in a short period of time. However, in the process of accumulating his great fortune, Stan saw his wife and two children leave home. He came to my office late one Thursday afternoon and told me several stories surrounding his moral compromises and failures. I can still remember his wet, blood-shot eyes staring at me as his broken voice sounded these emotional words: *"Is there hope for me?"*

I know that's the question that people want answered when they experience the brokenness of defeat. When personal ruin comes, is there light at the end of the tunnel? What does God offer me when I fall?

I know you're expecting an uplifting answer at this point. After all, pastors are supposed to offer optimism and hope to the hurting in their time of need. And certainly there are numerous Bible promises that can give consolation and encouragement when the going gets tough. But you don't see that *every* time. At least not in Judas' case. He was a failure and the Bible tells us he went out and killed himself. How encouraging is that? There must be a better answer than the standard reply, "There's hope for the hurting." What is it?

THE TWO ROADS FROM FAILURE

When you take more time to examine Judas' and Peter's life, you can see something significant that will give you a better perspective on failure. By watching their actions after their defeats, you discover that *failure can lead you two ways.* In other words, the answer to the question, "Is there hope?" is really a mixed bag. It can be "yes" or "no." It all depends on your attitude and your determination to deal with yourself after the defeat has occurred.

With Peter and Judas, God used their time of personal defeat to place them at a crossroads in their life. *This concept of a crossroads is the key.* They were divinely positioned to look back upon their previous failures in order to make a conscious decision about their lives. Either they would learn from their failures, make the necessary changes and grow from it or they would wallow in defeat and suffer the pain of not overcoming it. It's a matter of surrendering to the Holy Spirit's enabling. What did each person do?

Let's start with Judas. It says in Matthew 27:3, *"When Judas, who had betrayed him, saw that Jesus was condemned, he was seized with remorse and returned the thirty silver coins to the chief priests and the elders."* Judas' response revealed shallow *remorse.* He evidenced simple sorrow for what was done, but it wasn't enough to change him from the inside out. All he wanted to do was to go back and to correct the error. In his mind, he thought, "If I turn back the money, I'll get Jesus back and the problem will be resolved." However, the religious leaders didn't see it that way. They replied, *"What's that to us? That's your responsibility"* (Matthew 27:4b). Because of their answer, Judas realized that his failure could not be solved with a simple back step. He found himself in deep weeds. Because he was unwilling to deal with it squarely, he opted for the easy way out in the form of suicide.

There are many people today who look for the easy way out. They are sorry when they experience defeat, but it doesn't bother them *until they are caught.* When they are caught, you see them slide away from personal responsibility. In their thinking, the fault lies with other people, so they blame family members, friends and associates for their problems and failures. They will never admit that the real issue lies in their own life. They may not kill themselves like Judas, but they look for a way to evade the deficiencies revealed in their character. This is one road to failure. I call it the road of evasive responsibility.

Peter did something different in his response to failure. It says in Matthew 26:75, *"Then Peter remembered the word Jesus had spoken: 'Before the rooster crows, you will disown me three times.' And he went outside and wept bitterly."* The key idea in this text is the word *remember.* It's deeper than *remorse.* Peter recalled Jesus' words about his denial. His bitter weeping shows an intense repentance and deep sorrow over his behavior toward His Savior. He realized what he did and it drove him to a point of personal responsibility. Because he chose to deal with his actions, God brought healing into his life. He acknowledged his problems, went to the Lord for help and received the restoration to make him the spiritual leader who would feed God's sheep (John 21:15ff).

That's what God wants us to learn from failure in our lives. When we experience times of personal defeat, He places us at a crossroads in our life. We can choose to retreat from personal responsibility and end up in further decline or we can truly repent and receive God's healing to move on with life. The choice is ours. Deal with it now or let it slide into irresponsibility and personal decay.

FAILING FORWARD

So many powerful lessons can come to those who look failure straight in the eye and deal with it appropriately in their lives. Look at Peter. He was never the same after he faced the defeat from his denial. God used a dark experience in his life and transformed it into something beautiful. In a similar way, God wants us to see our failures as stepping stone opportunities to move us forward in our personal growth and development.

What lessons can you learn at the crossroads of failure? In Peter's case, he learned at least three. *The first lesson involved the depth of his sin.* At the end of Matthew 26:75, we see the emotional intensity from his denial experience. It says, *"He went outside and wept bitterly."* In his situation, he wasn't saddened just because he broke his promise to Christ (26:33-35). Rather, he felt something deeper. When he remembered the Lord's prophecy about his denial, it was as if a spiritual mirror appeared before his eyes. Instantly, he saw his pride, his arrogance and his self-centeredness flash before him as the religious authorities took Jesus away. When Peter gazed upon his true self, he became a broken man. This experience drove him to biblical sorrow, weeping and repentance.

Failure can show us the depth of our own sin in positive ways. I believe God ordains setbacks and defeats at important times in our life to humble us and to show us the true nature of our inner being. All too often, we tend to think that we're "OK" most of the time. We feed ourselves with strokes of self-centered affirmation and often we counsel ourselves to accept that our nature is basically good with a few slight shortcomings. Then we experience life-shattering consequences from our foolish acts and it truly shows what was there all along. Failure shows us the reality of our lives and it offers us an opportunity to see how badly we need Christ to change us from within.

The second lesson that Peter learned from failure is the restoration of God. I didn't see this lesson until recently when I was reading through the Gospel of Mark. Many times I had read Chapter 16, but two words stood out this time like never before. On that first Easter Sunday as the women entered the tomb and saw the young man dressed in a white robe, he told them not to fear but to know that Christ, the Savior had risen from the dead. After showing them the place where they laid Him, he says these significant words in verse 7, *"But go, tell his disciples **and Peter**, 'He is going ahead of you into Galilee. There you will see Him, just as He told you'"* (my emphasis). Did you see it? The two key words are "and Peter." In other words, Peter was singled out to receive a special word from the heavenly messenger. The women were to go and to tell the disciples and *especially Peter* that Christ had conquered death and hell, just as He promised.

There's powerful hope in those actions! Christ commissioned his messenger to tell the women to go to Peter with an affirming word of encouragement. In effect, the commission sounded something like this: "Women, go back to the disciples and especially to Peter, the one who betrayed me, and tell him that I have come back from the dead. Tell him this personally so that he will know that I love Him with a devoted love." Those two words "and Peter" reveal all this and much more from the text. When the future Apostle received it, he knew his relationship to Christ was restored because of the Lord's kindness and mercy. The same experience can also happen to you. You can look up to God and receive His restoration when you go through failure in your life. The key lies in knowing and responding to God's offer of reconciliation through repentance.

The third lesson Peter learned during his denial experience was that failure is not final. After all, look at his life after this event. He was never the same. Without question, this experience catapulted him to be one of the most significant leaders in the history of the first century church. How could a man who failed miserably by the world's own standard rise to such greatness? Let Peter give the answer, *"Praise be to the God and Father of our Lord Jesus Christ! In His great mercy He has given us new birth into a living hope through the resurrection of Jesus Christ from the dead, and into an inheritance that can never perish, spoil or fade—kept in heaven for you, who through faith are shielded by God's power until the coming of the salvation that is ready to be revealed in the last time"* (1 Peter 1:3-5). Peter received a living hope from his intimate communion with Christ. This hope gave him assurance to know that no matter how bad his failure looked, God was there to lift him up and to give him grace beyond his wildest imagination. Although he made himself a miserable wreck, God transformed him into a project of hope. And He can do it for you too!

How does your situation compare with Peter's account? Think about it. A man who denied the Lord of Glory three times wrote the verses we just saw from 1 Peter 1. He lied, compromised and distorted the truth about his personal friendship and relationship to Christ, his Master. *He got about as bad as one can get.* Yet despite his failure and hopeless situation, Christ was ready to take him and to lift him to a higher level by showing him that failure was not final in his life. Likewise in your life, Christ wants you to know that it doesn't matter how bad your failure looks before the world. If He can restore Peter, *He can restore you. Your failure is not final.* Listen to His voice and return to Him today.

SUMMARY

From Judas and Peter's life, we learn how personal defeat and failure strikes us often. God uses those times to put us at a crossroads to help us learn the depth of our sin as well as the hope of His mercy and restoration; however the key to seeing these lessons is your attitude and determination to deal with the defeats in your life. When you choose to acknowledge your sin and to allow God to break you in the ways that will promote healing and restoration, you'll learn that failure is not final in His plan for your life.

APPLICATION

Are you experiencing the pains of defeat today? Perhaps it's in your marriage, your family, your business, your relationships or your life in general. God has you where He wants you! Maybe you're at the crossroads of decision now. He wants you to turn to Him, learn from your brokenness and experience His restoration that comes from genuine repentance and confession. Will you allow Him to start a new beginning for your life today? It all depends on you!

PRAYER

Heavenly Father, I'm broken as I look upon the times that I failed you, others and myself. There are days when I feel like my life is a major defeat. I've made bad decisions, foolish errors and improper judgments at times and those things have hurt me. I've also let opportunities that would give me enrichment and fulfillment slip through my hands. Like Peter and Judas, I've broken my loyalty and witness to you and to others at critical times in my life. Today in your presence, I plead for forgiveness through the precious blood of Jesus. I seek your restoration and grace in my life. I know You have me at an important crossroads in my life. Today, I choose to turn to You. I want to receive the assurance of Your pardoning grace as well as the certainty of Your restoring touch in my heart. Take my life; it is Yours completely. Help me to see failure as a door to an endless hope as You lead me through this daily journey. Thank you for loving me more than I could ever love myself. I praise You for the truth that failure is not final. In the strong, restoring name of Jesus I pray. AMEN.

TALK TIME!

1. Think of the times when you experienced failure. How did you feel? How did you handle it?
2. "The world sees failure as a door to a hopeless end, whereas Christ sees failure as a door to an endless hope." Please discuss.
3. What are the most important things to remember when you're placed at the crossroads after failure?
4. Review the lessons Peter learned about failure. How can this encourage you?
5. Do you know someone who is experiencing the pains of defeat today? How can this lesson equip you to encourage them?

4

NO MORE WORRY WARTS

"You are worried and upset about many things"
Luke 10:41b

The Bureau of Standards in Washington, D.C. once released a scientific study on the nature of fog. Released in 1943,[9] it states, "A block of fog three feet wide, six feet high and one hundred feet long contains less than one-seventh of a glass of liquid water. This water is distributed among sixty billion drops." There isn't much substance in fog, yet its effects can be enormous. Even a small glass of water can produce drastic loss of vision for many people.

Isn't this a good picture of worry? A cupful of anxiety can go a long way in a person's life. Yet, when you analyze the nature and the substance of the things that "go bump in the night," often they carry little weight over the long haul.

A depressed, beaten old man sat in my office one day and told me what took the joy away from his life. He said, "I lost my happiness over the things of life that never occurred." Corrie ten Boom wrote, "Worry does not empty tomorrow of its sorrow; it empties today of its strength."[10] People in general and Christians in specific worry too much. We need to learn to handle worry more realistically in our lives.

How often do you worry? Are you the employer who always pulses with anxiety when you dream of everything that will go wrong on the job? Are you the parent who stews in fear over every

---

[9] W.J. Humphreys, *Fogs, Clouds and Aviation* (Baltimore: The Williams and Wilkins Company, 1943), p. 33. Obtained from the National Institute of Standards and Technology, Gaithersburg, Maryland.

[10] *Christian Herald* (June, 1981), p. 46.

aspect of your child's life? Are you the spouse who wonders if you're going to have enough money to pay the bills at the end of the month? Are you the student who lives in dread of your grades at school? So many people live today with tense hearts and sweaty hands because of worry. Are you one of them?

Many surveys have been done over the years to document the effects of worry in the general population. One that caught my attention was a Harris Poll entitled, "What will people die of in the future?"[11] The focus of the survey was to gain the general population's predictions for the major causes of death in the future. Astoundingly, majorities expect fewer people to die from most common diseases (cancers, diabetes, stroke and heart attack) while violent crime (guns, homicide) and will kill *more* people. In the report, Humphrey Taylor states, "The public is deeply pessimistic that guns, homicides, suicides and accident will kill more people in future and remarkably optimistic that fewer people will die from the diseases which kill most people now." This report tells us at least two things. First, people are greatly misinformed as to the causes of death in our society (heart disease still ranks number one overall). Second, media coverage of homicides from school gun shootings, shopping centers and suburban neighborhoods produce tremendous fear in people's hearts, especially parents for their children. Worry is alive and well in the world today.

Dr. Charles Mayo once said, "I have never known a man who died of hard work, but I do know many who died of worry."[12] Medical reports constantly remind us of the fatal consequences of uncontrollable worry. We need biblical wisdom to understand worry so that we can appropriate God's ways to conquer it in our life.

LESSON FOCUS

When we decide through conviction and prayer to let God control the people and circumstances of our lives instead of ourselves, we will hand over the concerns and baggage that daily plague us to the Lord and let His Spirit guard our hearts and minds in the

---

[11] Poll #2, January 13, 2000. Go to www.harrisinteractive.com

[12] John MacArthur, *Anxiety Attacked (Chariot Victor Publishing*, 1993), chapter 1.

Word of God.

WHAT IS WORRY?

Our English word "worry" comes from the old German word *Wurgen* which means, "to choke." As it was used through the centuries, it came to denote the "choking of the mind" or "mental strangulation." It described the condition of a person whose life was gripped and constricted with anxiety and fear. It shows where many people live today. Their fixated thoughts about the things of the past, present and future sap them of the needed strength to face the opportunities for today. Because worry chokes so many people, a day focused on these kinds of tensions becomes more exhausting than a whole month of work.

What is the root problem of worry? What makes people so afraid? From my observations, I sense that *a central issue surrounding worry is control.* The things we cannot master and control become the things that direct us and move us in many ways. When people allow the issues of this life to control them, they face intense times of insecurity and instability. Haddon Robinson summarized it well when he said, "What worries you masters you."[13] Today, many individuals live under the control of other people, past failures and missed opportunities. When they dwell on these kinds of worldly controls in their life, flashes of uncontrollable uncertainties supplant God's design for their life, sending them quickly to emotional and spiritual paralysis.

KITCHEN WORRY VERSUS LIVING ROOM DEVOTION

A good picture of worry comes from Martha's kitchen in Luke 10. In this account, Martha opened her home to the Lord with gracious hospitality. Her sister Mary was expected to assist her in all the necessary preparations for the occasion; however Mary chose to listen at the Lord's feet (10:39), frustrating Martha more with each passing minute.

---

[13] Haddon Robinson, *Good News Broadcaster*, April 1978, p. 7.

In desperation, Martha went to Jesus, asking Him to persuade Mary to help her. It is assumed that she had asked Mary several times for kitchen help with no apparent success. As the situation became more uncontrollable, she went to Jesus for relief. Sensing her tension, the Lord reminded Martha that Mary's decision was the correct one. Mary's thoughts centered on the Lord's presence whereas Martha's mind was mastered by the events that she couldn't control.

What's mastering you today? Worry comes when we seek to control things that God never intended us to control. With Martha, Christ never meant for her to become consumed with kitchen duty. He didn't want her to control the events of the home. Rather, He wanted both sisters to enjoy His fellowship by delighting in His presence. In His thinking, the most important action in their home was to develop wholesome relationships, not emotional control through perfectionism. Something was mastering Martha, and it kept her from the Lord. Likewise, if something is mastering you today, you can't enjoy the fullness of Christ's presence the way He wants you to experience it. You're stuck in your worrisome kitchen while Christ is waiting for you in the living room. Get out of the kitchen! Take off your apron and sit for a spell!

COMMON WORRIES

There is an old proverb that says, "Blessed is the man who is too busy to worry in the daytime and too tired to worry at night." It is unfortunate that so many practice this principle in reverse. I've met hosts of people that are too occupied with their fears at night and too tired to handle the challenges of the day. What are the common worries that rattle people?

For some, worry comes *from their past*. In their life, the recurring thoughts of a secret mistake or a sin committed in earlier years bring terror and fear to their emotional life. Many people, Christians included, are haunted day and night by these mental road markers from the past. They fear that the resurrection and revelation of these buried and submerged practices will bring devastation and embarrassment to personal and family life. People in this category sometimes spend great amounts of time, money and concentration to insure that these hideous chapters of their lives never come forth from the grave.

Lana (name changed) comes to my mind when I think of people that fall into this category. She was a sweet, caring older person in the church. Everyone knew her and appreciated all the volunteer hours that she gave for the pastor in phone calling and in hospital visitation. Since I was overseeing volunteer ministry at the time, I saw her every Wednesday morning, checking the visitation rolls and scheduling shepherding visits for the pastors to the sick and to the bereaved; however, one morning, her countenance was troubled. She asked to speak to me in my office. As she sat down, uncontrollable tears began to flow.

"I've held something in my life for many years," she said. "It's been controlling me for too long, and I need deliverance from it." I asked her to tell me what was on her heart. After a brief pause and a word of confidential assurance from me, she said, "I had an abortion back in the days when abortions were considered wrong. My husband was away in the Korean War, so he never knew about it. But I've carried it all my life. You're the first person I've ever told about this. I need help."

I grieved with Lana that day. I saw how she lacked understanding to appropriate God's full forgiveness in her personal life. I assured her that the Lord provided a full and free pardon based upon Christ's death on the Cross. Because of His accomplishment, the penalty for our failures has been paid. God has forgiven us completely and totally. Sins of the past are removed as far as the east is from the west (Psalm 103:12). Because of our union with Christ, there is no condemnation (Romans 8:1). The past is covered and God says, *"Your sins I will remember no more"* (Jeremiah 31:34). For the Christian, the worries of the past have received Jesus' stamp of pardon. They are signed, sealed and forgiven by Him.

A second group of worries centers in the *concerns of the present.* Those who live in this category feel that day-to-day living resembles a rat race. They are fearful of the demands of daily life, wondering whether they will be able to keep up with the expectations and standards that are around them. For many, money is a centerpiece in this picture. Questions like "Do I have enough?" "Will I ever have enough?" "Will it continue to be enough?" voice common concerns that itch away at the minds of those who feel like they are behind the proverbial eight ball of life.

Jim and Claudia (names changed) fall into this category. Every time you talked to them, there was never enough money in the bank account. Every time Jim walked into church, he would exhale deep breaths of weariness. He worked hard and long hours as a restaurant manager, yet never felt that he carried home a sufficient paycheck. He was never able to finish college because they had four kids born many years apart. Because of this, Claudia wanted to stay home as the glue of the family, but Jim mounted continued pressure to nudge her back to work as a public accountant. The more Claudia refused, the higher the tensions became in the house. I recall a time after Wednesday night church when Claudia came to me privately and expressed the worries and fears from this continued pressure on her life. "I'm supposed to submit, pastor, but I don't feel it's right," she said. "What do I do?"

There are thousands of women like Claudia facing these kinds of daily pressures in the home. Let me make myself clear at this point. We've all seen situations where it is necessary for women to work to keep the house financially afloat. At the same time, I've also seen occasions where these kinds of tensions are steeped in greed and jealousy. There are homes with young children where one spouse pressures the other spouse to work so that they can keep up with the neighbors next door or the rising family in the country club. Those that fall into this latter category ignore God's promise to meet all the provisions of the present. Paul declared, *"My God shall meet all your needs according to His riches and glory in Christ Jesus"* (Philippians 4:19). The issue lies in dependence upon God to supply our daily needs. Will we trust God or will we rely on our own efforts to bring satisfaction and contentment? Remember this about the rat race: *even if you win it, you're still a rat.*

A third group of worries comes from *a tense fixation on the future.* Parents have this when they think of the future of their children. Others are gravely concerned about their job security and retirement accounts. People express fear that they will live a long life or experience premature death because of illness or accident. These kinds of worries center on the uncertainties of life and the futile attempts to control them.

Jesus spoke often about this kind of worry. *"Therefore do not worry about tomorrow, for tomorrow will worry about itself. Each day has enough trouble of its own"* (Matthew 6:34). This kind of anxiety will not add a single hour to a person's life (Matthew 6:27). It leads only to futility and to a never-ending cycle of tension and fear.

D.W. Whittle penned a significant poem that speaks to this issue:

> I have nothing to do with tomorrow;
> It's sunlight I may never see.
> So today, with the plow in the furrow,
> In the vineyard I faithful would be.
>
> I have nothing to do with tomorrow;
> My Savior will make that His care,
> Its grace and its strength I can't borrow.
> So why should I borrow its care?[14]

We have enough to think about today. We can't change yesterday. Tomorrow is hours away. God has told us not to worry! But how do you do it?

PUTTING WORRY IN ITS PLACE

A.W. Tozer hit the ball soundly when he wrote, "The best way to control our thoughts is to offer the mind to God in complete surrender. The Holy Spirit will accept it and take control of it immediately.[15] That *sounds* like a good thing to do. But how do you do it?

God's Word gives us specific steps to help us conquer worry in our lives. These steps form principles that can enable us to handle the fears and troubles that seek to strangle us emotionally and spiritually.

The first step is conviction. I must come to the place where I know that worry is wrong for my life. I must realize that it will not help me, nor will it enrich my life. Instead, I must come to the firm resolution that God does not want my mind to dwell on all the uncontrollable uncertainties that can paralyze my spiritual well being. Paul wrote, *"Do not be anxious about anything.."* (Philippians 4:6a). It

---

[14] D.W. Whittle, *Pentecostal Evangel.* (May 21, 1978), p. 3.
[15] Warren W. Wiersbe, *The Best of A.W. Tozer* (Baker, 1978), p. 45.

means exactly what it says. *Stop worrying.* Realize its harm. Understand that it will not help you. Write a will on your worry. Contact the funeral home director of your mind. Christ wants you to call in the hearse. It's time to lower worry's casket into the grave!

The second step in conquering worry is to hand over the baggage officially. God wants these unnecessary burdens and scars lifted from your life and placed upon Him. Peter wrote, *"Cast all your anxiety on Him because He cares for you"* (I Peter 5:7). This step is necessary in order to receive the lasting kind of victory over worry that God wants to give you.

Many times Christians do this and receive periodic victories in this effort; however Satan comes in at that point and brings opposition and circumstances to bear that can elevate the tension level of your life. That's why this step demands that we deliberately decide *to let God control the uncertainties that lurk before us and not ourselves.* Remember that worry comes from improper worldly control. Let Christ take your cares, your worries and your unknowns. By giving them over to Him, you are saying, *"God, I am no longer in control. You are."*

The third step in conquering worry comes from Scriptural meditation. Paul told the Philippian christians that the way God brings peace and contentment is through Scriptural thinking (Philippians 4:8). Thoughts that are true, pure, noble, lovely and excellent bring rest to the inner world because they reiterate to us that God is in charge of our lives. How do you get these kinds of biblical thoughts? By reading and meditating upon God's Word!

Scripture memory and meditation continues to get a bad rap these days. Many people claim that it is not a necessary part of the Christian walk. I've heard people say, "It's good for those whose minds are alert and clear, but not essential for me." This thinking illustrates the kind of laziness that infiltrates the church of our times. Paul told us that godliness comes though training (I Timothy 4:7-8). Sure, Scripture memory takes work and discipline! But so does listening to new music, playing sports and watching movies! It's all a matter of determination and concentration. Remember this: *you spend time on what you think is valuable.*

This step demands that a regular, disciplined Bible reading and memory program occupy your weekly time schedule. Get out your weekly planner and schedule time not just to read God's Word, *but also to meditate and to memorize it.* When the mind is filled regularly with the truths of Scripture, thoughts of fear and worry will run away. You'll be constantly reminded that God is in charge of your world and your life. In the end, you'll feel better, think better and rest better knowing that God will do a much better job than anyone else could!

The fourth step that follows Scriptural meditation is consistent prayer. Paul also reminded the Philippian believers that the opposite of anxiety was a committed prayer life. He wrote, *"Do not be anxious about anything, but in everything, by prayer and petition, with thanksgiving, present your requests to God. And the peace of God, which transcends all understanding, will guard your hearts and your minds in Christ Jesus"* (Philippians 4:6-7). We gain lasting victory over anxiety when we pray about everything in the knowledge of Scripture. Fear will never calm our troubles, but prayer will.

Recent personal conversations with Christian leaders seem to indicate why many professing believers worry too much in their lives. From their own congregations and Christian organizations, they have shared how many of their people admit to spending an average of *just two minutes a day in prayer.* It's no wonder that many of them are cracking up today! They have failed to go to the source of peace and contentment in daily life. Personal prayer and corporate prayer in the body of Christ acknowledge the Holy Spirit as the leader of our lives. When we rest in His empowerment and direction, He removes the fears and anxieties from our hearts. But this kind of rest will come only as we take the time to do it. Again, get out your weekly planner and schedule it as a high priority. Priority in prayer will produce progress over worry.

SUMMARY

We have reviewed the causes and kinds of worry, learning basic steps needed to conquer it in our private lives. If the tension of our inner world is not checked and removed, it will paralyze our lives and threaten our spiritual well being. God's Word has much to say about the dangers of worry. You can receive practical help from the

Holy Spirit to drive away worry and to remove its warts from your mind. But the question remains. Will you?

APPLICATION

What's controlling you today? What goes "bump" in your night? Are you biting your fingernails? Losing sleep? Feeling tense and helpless? God has you right where He wants you! Decide in your heart *right now* that you're going to give up control. Live by conviction that Jesus is in charge of this entire world, including your life. Hand over the heavy baggage to Him and start spending time in Bible reading, memorization and prayer. Then go to bed and let Him handle the issues of your life. He wants to do it for you! Why won't you let Him?

PRAYER

Lord Jesus, I'm driving home a spiritual stake in my soul today. I'm deliberately declaring that worry will not control me any more in my life. The things of the past, present and future are laid at Your Cross. I give all the baggage of my inner world into Your hands. I want You to take charge and to control my life. Give me a hunger to concentrate and to meditate upon Your Word. Fill my mind with the comforting thoughts of Scripture. I ask for the peace that passes all understanding. Use it to guard my heart and my mind while I rest on Your strength to carry me through the day. Help me to put the past to rest, to wait for the future and to concentrate on the blessings that I have today. Throughout this day and the days to come, help me to come to You regularly in prayer to receive the peace that You provide. Thank you for the way You want to care for me. I make this commitment to You. In Your precious Name I pray. AMEN.

TALK TIME!

1. How often do you worry? What are the things that go "bump in the night" for you?
2. Do you think more people worry about the past, the present or the future? Why?

3. What are the signs that visibly indicate you're in a state of worry?
4. Look again at the account of Martha and Mary in Luke 10. Who do you identify with more—Mary or Martha?
5. Review the Scriptural principles for putting worry in its place. In your experience, which one is the easiest to do? Which is the most difficult? Why?
6. Do you know someone who is worrying today? How can this lesson equip you to help him/her?

5

HELP! I NEED GUIDANCE!

*"In all your ways acknowledge Him, and He will
make your paths straight."*
Proverbs 3:6

People do the strangest things to get guidance these days. Perhaps you heard the story of the stressed-out college student who was finishing his senior year with no direction where he would go after graduation. He occasionally read His Bible and felt compelled one morning to open it for help. He pondered where he would look to get the answers he needed. The more he thought, the more confused he became. All of a sudden, an idea struck him, propelling him to action.

With his eyes closed, he opened his Bible and placed his finger on the page. The verse that appeared under his finger would be God's will for his life. With this game plan, he proceeded with haste and anticipation.

On his first turn, he was stunned to discover these words about Judas when he opened his eyes: *"Then he went away and hanged himself"* (Matthew 27:5b). Convinced that it was just an unfortunate draw, he proceeded to do it a second time, confident of better results. He closed his eyes, opened his Bible, placed his finger on the page, then read these surprising words in Luke 10:37b, *"Go and do likewise."* He pondered to himself, "Are these connected?" Shrugging off any relationship between the two, he decided to try for a third and final time. He looked with bewilderment when his eyes opened and saw these words from John 13:27b, *"What you are about to do, do quickly."* Like many people, he walked away shaking his head, wondering if he would ever get the wisdom he needed.

You won't find guidance with that procedure! God doesn't offer haphazard, blind tours through His Word. Instead, He has given us sufficient help to guide us through the issues we face in life with wisdom when we really need it the most. The key is learning these principles and building biblical perspective and maturity through them.

Although God directs us step by step through the events of our lives, at times you can't see it in the here and now. Sometimes it's only when we pause to look back and see where we've come, recollecting the circumstances and the people that were in our path, that we begin to sense a divine leading in our life. When we take stock of the broad picture of our lives, we begin to sense that somehow, for some reason, we've gone from this place to that place under the influence of a mysterious director. It's easier to see God's guidance and direction as you look back. But can you get it when you look forward?

LESSON FOCUS

You can receive God's guidance for your life when you understand what God wants you to be in His sight. The more you understand your identity in Christ, the more enabled you will be to use His tools to discern the directions in life you are to take. Use His resources with faith and patience, listening to His Holy Spirit's voice as you watch God's activity ahead of you.

FIRST, IT'S AN ISSUE OF BEING

Too often, people seeking guidance want a reasonably proven step by step formula that will wave a spiritual wand over their future, giving them the knowledge they seek. After all, many see the infomercials about the psychic readers offering a free consultation and they think this can apply to the Christian life. Who can blame them when they see the way some professing Christians act these days?

First and foremost, Christianity is not a program or method. Instead, *it's an intimate relationship with the Living God.* Only true believers can receive God's guidance. *It's an issue of being.* Don't think that you can live the kind of life you want to live and receive God's direction in return. It won't work that way. You must be a child of God first through a personal relationship with Jesus Christ. When you become a Christian through conversion (John 3), you are changed from the inside. The former way of life is past. You're given a new life. Your affections and interests are different. Instead of following the ways of the world, you're pursuing the things of Christ with devotion and passion. You are becoming a new person from the inside out.

When you receive this spiritual transformation, you are immediately joined in an intimate relationship with Christ. Jesus likened the connection to a vine and its branches (John 15). This intimacy produces a thirst for God. As you grow in your relationship to Christ, you seek to become a person after God's own heart. When your inner life longs for God's presence and favor, you will receive the wisdom and guidance you need.

In his early adult life, Solomon pursued God with all his heart and gained His wisdom in return. 2 Chronicles 1:7-12 records his sincerity before God:

> *"That night God appeared to Solomon and said to him, 'Ask for whatever you want me to give you.' Solomon answered God, 'You have shown great kindness to David my father and have made me king in his place. Now, Lord God, let your promise to my father David be confirmed, for you have made me king over a people who are as numerous as the dust of the earth. Give me wisdom and knowledge, that I may lead this people, for who is able to govern this great people of yours?'"*

Listen to Solomon's heart as he asks for wisdom. He had the right intent. God commended him for not seeking wealth, long life or victory over his enemies. The young king's heart was right with God, and his motives were sincere and transparent. That's what God's person looks like on the inside. He/she is an individual after His own heart.

BECOMING A PERSON AFTER GOD'S OWN HEART

Solomon is not a unique biblical example. Many people in the Scriptures pursued God. They longed to have a heart like His. How did they get there? What is involved in becoming spiritually passionate, focused on the things of God?

First, it means dedicating your life to God. Paul exhorted the Christians in Rome to do this, *"Therefore, I urge you, brothers, in view of God's mercy, to offer your bodies as living sacrifices, holy and pleasing to God—which is your spiritual worship. Do not be conformed any longer to the pattern of this world, but be transformed by the renewing of your mind. Then you will be able to test and approve what God's will is—his good, pleasing and perfect will"* (Romans 12:1-2). Becoming a person after God's heart means offering your life in complete consecration to Him. Don't let anything get in the way between you and the Lord.

When I think of consecration to the Lord, I'm drawn to the life of George Müeller of Bristol. God used him to establish orphan houses simply by faith in the promises of Scripture with no advertising or public announcements for money. How could be do this? Müeller wrote:

> Now if I, a poor man, simply by prayer and faith, obtained, without asking any individual, the means for establishing and carrying on an orphan house, there would be something which, with the Lord's blessing, might be instrumental in strengthening the faith of the children of God, besides being a testimony to the consciences of the unconverted of the reality of the things of God. This, then, was the primary reason for establishing the orphan house. I certainly did from my heart desire to be used by God to benefit the bodies of poor children bereaved of both parents, and seek, in order respects, with the help of God, to do them good for this life;—I also particularly longed to be used by God in getting the dear orphans trained up in the fear of God;—but still, the first and primary object of the work was (and still is) that God might be magnified by the fact that the orphans under my care are provided with all they need only by prayer and faith, without any one being asked by me or my fellow labourers, whereby it may be seen that God is faithful and hears prayer still .[16]

Are you willing to be a person after God's own heart? It starts with a total, obedient dependence to the Lord Jesus Christ, the supplier of our every need. Are you ready to take the plunge? Think how much power Christ could have in your life when you make this commitment!

The second step in becoming a person after God's heart is to make God the delight of your life. Psalm 37:4 states, *"Delight yourself in the Lord and He will give you the desires of your heart."* Are you dedicating your life to God, pursuing Him as the passion of your soul? Talk to Him regularly. Let Him love you with His overflowing affection. Make Him the first love of your heart. When you do this, amazing things begin to happen in your life. You start to see things differently. God gives you desires and delights that reflect His will for your life. As you set your affection on Him, these desires will come, building a greater trust in your spirit.

Frederick Faber (1814-1863), one of my favorite hymn writers, showed this kind of delight in his writings:

> My God, how wonderful Thou art
> Thy majesty how bright,
> How beautiful Thy mercy seat,
> In depths of burning light!
>
> How wonderful, how beautiful
> The sight of Thee must be,
> Thine endless wisdom, boundless power,
> And awful purity![17]

Delighting in God means thinking about Him—His character, actions and attributes.

The third step in becoming a person after God's heart is to trust God's plan for your life. Proverbs 3:5-6 says, *"Trust in the Lord with all your heart and lean not on your own understanding; in all your ways acknowledge him, and he will make your paths straight."* God has a plan for your life. The key to discovering it is to trust Him

---

[16]Arthur Pierson, *George Müeller of Bristol.* (Revell), p. 398.

[17] Frederick Faber, "My God, How Wonderful Thou Art" in *Worship and Service Hymnal* (Hope Publishing, 1968), #4.

with the details while you walk with Him. Trust is the foundation for growth in the Christian life.

I remember a time when a church that I had recently planted was praying about buying a strategic piece of land just a half a mile from the interstate. There was tension in the air over this development. Should we step out in faith and claim this land for God's kingdom or were we acting foolish, not showing any common sense? I looked at this familiar passage late one night and agonized over what to do in leading the church at that moment. Should we buy the land or let it go? As I pondered, I asked myself some pertinent questions. God gave me some significant thoughts for that moment.

WHAT DOES "TRUST IN THE LORD" REALLY MEAN?

- Trust is an attitude of the heart, like the child that brought five loaves and two fishes to the disciples for Jesus to feed the multitudes (John 6).
- Trust is the desire to see God act in ways I can't predict.
- Trust is accepting the future from a voice that says, "I'm in charge."
- Trust is the willingness to place my life in God's hands for everything.
- When I'm surrendering my ambitions and goals to God's ultimate purpose for my life, I'm trusting Him.

WHAT DOES "WITH ALL YOUR HEART" REALLY MEAN?

- The heart is the core of life. It is my being, my convictions and my essence.
- God is saying to me, "I don't want your things. I want you!"
- This means it's not *part* of my life. It's *all* of it!
- I can't trust God using logic and rational thought. God says, "Trust me with all your *heart*, not just your head."

- It's from my heart that the issues of life come (Proverbs 4:23).
- My heart speaks of my purest intent and passion.

WHAT DOES "DO NOT LEAN UPON YOUR OWN UNDERSTANDING" REALLY MEAN?

- Sometimes Satan's greatest tool is my own rationalism and ambition.
- I want to think in my own ways based on my own experiences.
- God is above all these experiences. My thoughts and understanding are not God's thoughts and understanding.
- I'm commanded *not to lean*. To go God's way, I can't depend on my ability to think things through. I must look to Him for answers.
- My understanding is limited. God's is unlimited.

WHAT DOES "IN ALL YOUR WAYS ACKNOWLEDGE HIM" REALLY MEAN?

- It means in every stage of my life (child, youth adult).
- In every dimension of my life (work, family, play).
- In every step of my journey through life.
- Whatever I do, do it all for the glory of God (1 Corinthians 10:31).
- Remember that He is the source of true wisdom.

WHAT DOES "HE WILL MAKE YOUR PATHS STRAIGHT" REALLY MEAN?

- It means He will show me great and mighty things I

don't know currently (Jeremiah 33:3).
- Before I see the straight path, there is a price to pay. The cost is trust.
- "Paths" is plural. It is a continuous cycle through my life.
- Since He will make His ways plain to me if I trust Him and not myself, what would I attempt for God, knowing that I wouldn't fail if He was in it?

The fourth step in becoming a person after God's heart is to do what He has already stated in His Word. Obedience shows the outer world that your inner world is in order. What are some of God's clear commands? Let's list a few of them:

- Holiness in sexuality (1 Thessalonians 4:3).
- Thanks in all circumstances (1 Thessalonians 5:18).
- Submission to governing authorities (1 Peter 2:15).
- Justice and mercy (Micah 6:8).
- Tithes to your local church (Malachi 3:10).
- Contentment with what you have (Hebrews 13:5).

Some people have the unfounded idea that God will come near them and bless them with guidance when they don't do what He's already told them to do. The Psalmist writes, *"If I had cherished sin in my heart, the Lord would not have listened"* (Psalm 66:18). When you obey God, you start to become a person after His own heart.

This first principle of receiving God's guidance by becoming a person after His own heart is a daily process, starting right now. Patrick Morley wrote, "Jesus said, 'If you love me, obey me.' In other words, 'If you want to demonstrate to Me in a tangible way that I am pre-eminent in you, then live up to the Truth you have already received. Anyone can say they love Me, but the one who lives up to what they have already attained pleases God. And that doesn't happen yesterday or tomorrow—it happens in the now.'"[18]

---

[18] Patrick Morley, *I Surrender: Submitting to Christ in the Details of Life* (Wolgemuth and Hyatt, 1990), p. 105.

SECOND, LOOK AT GOD'S TOOLBOX

If you are experiencing a vital, meaningful relationship with God, joined to Jesus Christ because of His death and resurrection, you can call God "your Father" (Romans 8:15). With this special relationship, you can appreciate the resources that only He can give to guide you in your journey through life.

Only true believers can receive God's inner guidance. Don't try to think that you can live the kind of life you want to live and receive God's direction at the same time. It won't work that way. You must know God through a personal relationship with Christ. When you do, the Lord offers significant resources to give you direction in life.

The first resource in His toolbox is the knowledge of His Word. The Psalmist writes, *"Your word is a lamp to my feet and a light to my path"* (Psalm 119:105). The Apostle Paul encouraged the believers at Rome to use the Word of God to build up one another in knowledge and in hope. He wrote, *"For everything that was written in the past was written to teach us, so that through endurance and the encouragement of the Scriptures we might have hope* (Romans 15:4). It's not enough to *have* a Bible. You must *use* it daily to learn more about God and about His will for your life. The *knowledge* of God's Word is the point I'm making here. There is no substitute for maturing in your understanding of the Bible's message. This will give you perspective as you spend time reading and studying it daily.

John Murray, beloved Professor of Systematic Theology at Westminster Seminary wrote these significant words encouraging us to diligent Bible study:

> Painstaking study of the Bible is indispensable to our own thought and practice. Life is very complex and we are constantly beset with baffling questions. New situations daily confront us. If the situations are not entirely new, old situations take on new colour and new settings. We need to know anew what is the right thing to think and what is the right thing to do. If we are to meet these situations, we must be armed with the Sword of the Spirit which is the Word of God, and we must be equipped with

> such knowledge of the Word that we shall derive from it
> the needed direction and strength.[19]

The Bible is the first tool needed to receive God's direction and perspective once your heart is fixed upon Him.

The second resource in God's toolbox is the ministry of His Holy Spirit. Jesus promised His disciples that the Spirit of God would come as a counselor to them (John 14 and 15). The Apostle Paul wrote, *"The Spirit himself testifies with our spirit that we are God's children...In the same way, the Spirit helps us in our weakness. We do not know what we ought to pray, but the Spirit himself intercedes for us with groans that words cannot express"* (Romans 8:16,26). As our lifelong guide and friend, the Holy Spirit reveals to us the mind of Christ and shows us the paths that God wants us to take. Our daily responsibility is to seek His filling (Ephesians 5:18b) so that we can hear Him speak clearly to us. This means living under His leadership and staying in sync with His direction in our lives (Galatians 5:25).

D. Martyn Lloyd Jones wrote, "The moment a man is born again and this divine seed or principle enters into him, the life has started and there is this imperceptible growth. But let a man like that be baptized with the Holy Spirit, let the rain and the sunshine of the Spirit come upon him, let the love of God be shed abroad in his heart, and you will see him springing up into life and vigour and activity; his sanctification, everything about him, is stimulated in a most amazing and astonishing manner."[20] This kind of stimulation is available to those seeking guidance and direction in life. When you ask for God's Spirit in faith and in obedience, you receive power and hope for living.

The third resource in God's toolbox is the counsel of His people. Proverbs 11:14 states, *"For lack of guidance a nation falls, but many advisors make victory sure."* One chapter later, Solomon wrote, *"The way of a fool seems right to him, but a wise man listens to advice"* (12:15). As you faithfully build your maturity in the Word of God and consecrate your life to the indwelling of the Holy Spirit, seek the wisdom and knowledge of other people, especially those who have

---

[19] John Murray, *Collected Writings: Volume 1* (Banner of Truth, 1976), p. 6.
[20] D. Martyn Lloyd-Jones, *Joy Unspeakable* (Harold Shaw, 1984), pp. 143-144.

gone through similar experiences in their lives. The key issue in this step is *timing*. Do all you can to search the Scriptures and to listen to the Holy Spirit within you. *Then* seek the advice of other godly men and women in your life. Proverbs 25:11 says, *"A word aptly spoken is like apples of gold in settings of silver."*

Elisabeth Elliot wrote, "God works always with perfect wisdom, always with perfect love, and nearly always in conjunction with human means."[21] Look around you. Find two or three people at the most whom you believe can help you with an issue you're facing. Then talk to them. Listen to their counsel. Ask them as many questions as you can. Let the Holy Spirit confirm or dismiss their thoughts about your situation. When you accept legitimate instruction from another person, you will receive helpful guidance along the way. Proverbs 19:20 says, *"Listen to advice and accept instruction, and in the end you will be wise."*

A fourth resource in God's toolbox is the appearance of divine activity around you. In other words, when you sense God's providential arrangement of circumstances and people moving you in a specific course, it could possibly indicate God's direction for your life. There are times when you can observe God's work happening all around you. His work itself is a tool that can lead you with needed guidance. This activity confirms Jesus' words in John 5:17, *"My Father is always at His work to this very day, and I, too, am working."*

Notice where I put this resource in the list. It's at the end for a good reason. Too often, circumstances and activity can be misleading. We misinterpret events and occurrences as God's handwriting on the walls when sufficient time has not elapsed for proper evaluation and review. Look at Peter in Acts 10. He sees many signs of God's providential working all around him, yet he makes no conclusions until he reaches Cornelius' home. Then he understands that God sent him to usher the gospel to the Gentiles. He didn't make a premature conclusion. He let God's activity lead him, then the answers came in the proper time. Likewise, focus your energies on the first three resources (Bible, Holy Spirit and godly counsel).

---

[21] Elisabeth Elliot, *A Slow and Certain Light* (Word, 1973), p. 96.

They will help you discern God's providential actions.

Now that these resources have received sufficient overview, it's important to understand the way God wants us to use them in seeking His guidance for the important decisions in our lives. What kind of life pleases God and gives Him pleasure?

THIRD, COME TO GOD IN FAITH

God gives guidance to those who come to Him in trust and absolute surrender. Hebrews 11:6 says, *"And without faith it is impossible to please God, because anyone who comes to Him must believe that He exists and that He rewards those who earnestly seek Him."* When we approach God with a heart that is sincere before Him, combining this with an unwavering trust in His plan, the writer to the Hebrews says *God rewards* those who seek Him. From my observations, one of His rewards is guidance.

Commenting on Hebrews 11:6, J. Gresham Machen wrote, "In the first place, religion is here made to depend absolutely upon doctrine; the one who comes to God must not only believe *in* a person, but he must also believe *that* something is true; faith is here declared to involve acceptance of a proposition. There could be no plainer insistence upon the doctrinal or intellectual basis of faith. It is impossible, according to the Epistle to the Hebrews, to have faith in a person without accepting with the mind the facts about the person."[22] Machen's words are right on target. You can't believe in someone you haven't met and you can't trust that person without first hand knowledge. A few verses earlier in Hebrews 11, the writer stated that faith is content, conviction and certainty that the things said about God in His Word are true (11:1). This means factual knowledge and personal experience. You can't please God without knowing Him and you can't receive his direction unless you come to Him.

FAITH'S EXPRESSION

How do you come to God in faith? When you're seeking guidance and direction, what will faith look like? How is trust seen when

---

[22] J. Gresham Machen, *What is Faith?* (Eerdmans, 1925), p. 47.

you approach God for help?

The first way faith is expressed is in Christ-centered confidence. Hebrews 10:19 says, *"Therefore, brothers, since we have **confidence** to enter the Most High Place by the blood of Jesus, by a new and living way opened for us through the curtain, that is His body, and since we have a great priest over the house of God, let us draw near to God with a sincere heart in full assurance of faith"* (my emphasis). If you truly believe that God is your loving Heavenly Father because of the work of Christ, you will not feel bashful in approaching Him with certainty and boldness. Jesus made it possible for you to come directly to God. Go straight to the source! Ask the Father with confidence because of Jesus' work!

This confidence is best seen in prayer. Andrew Murray wrote, "Prayer is the very essence of true religion, the channel of all blessings, and the secret of power and life. Not only for ourselves, but also for others—for the church, for the world—it is to prayer that God has given the right to take hold of Him and His strength."[23] Your prayer life will reveal to a great degree the confidence level you have in God.

The second way faith is expressed is in patience. Many times faith is seen when you acknowledge that God's timing is always right and that He never fails to lead you in straight directions at the right time. David wrote in Psalm 40:1, *"I waited patiently for the Lord; He turned to me and heard my cry."* He also said, *"Wait for the Lord; be strong and take heart and wait for the Lord"* (Psalm 27:14). When you evidence patience in God's sovereign plan, your trust level will build, providing you with endurance to submit to His direction for your life.

John Piper wrote, "Patience is the capacity to 'wait and to endure' without murmuring and disillusionment—to wait in the unplanned place, and endure the unplanned pace."[24] Remember the lesson about the oyster and the grain of sand. It never feels good when you're in the tough times, but the moments you choose to stick it out and to endure with patience will be the times when the greatest

---

[23] Andrew Murray, *Lord, Teach Us to Pray* booklet (Bible Pathway Ministries, Murfreesboro, TN), p. 3-4.

[24] John Piper, *Living By Faith in Future Grace* (Multnomah, 1995), p. 172.

jewels will come your way. Keep on working at being a person after God's own heart. Use the resources in His toolbox. While all this is going on, wait in confidence expectation that God will guide you at the right time. He always has and always will!

SUMMARY

During the times that you need guidance for the important decisions in your life, remember that God wants you to be *His* person *first* before you receive His guidance. Work on your personal relationship with Christ. Make Him the delight of your life.

Dedicate yourself unreservedly to Him by trusting completely in His plan for your future. Make obedience to His revealed Word a central priority in your daily operation. When you concentrate on *being* God's person, He will give you tools such as His Word, His Spirit, His people and His providential actions to guide you. While you watch Him work, live with patience and confidence, trusting His timing and His plan. You'll get the guidance and counsel you need to make the next step.

APPLICATION

Are you God's person today? Can someone say about you, "He/she is a person after God's own heart?" Knowledge and wisdom come from the fear of the Lord (Proverbs 1:7). Will you make the effort to dedicate your life to Him? You can't discern what His good, pleasing and perfect will is until you consecrate yourself to His care (Romans 12:2b).

Been in God's toolbox lately? How sharp is your knowledge of His Word? Are you building biblical maturity? Is your knowledge growing? Can you hear the voice of the Holy Spirit speaking to you at times? He wants to help you in your time of need!

Think of two trusted friends whom you can call when you need guidance about something. Take them out to lunch and glean their wisdom and experience. God uses people in His sovereign plan to help you along the way. Finally, watch what God is doing around you. Wait patiently for Him to show His ways to you. When you live in confidence and in faith, He will guide you and show you the path you are to go. And while you're traveling down the road looking for more light, enjoy the ride. The journey is as much fun as the final destination.

PRAYER

Heavenly Father, I need your guidance today. My world hovers in a state of confusion most of the time. I know it's because I've failed to grow in my relationship to You. Today, I dedicate myself unreservedly to Your watchful care. I'm putting You first in everything I do. Give me Your heart to see the world like You see it. Help me to delight in Your ways. Give me the faith to trust You and not my own rational thought. May Your Comforter, the Holy Spirit, rule in my life and lead me in Your paths of righteousness. Thank You for the fantastic tools you offer to give me direction for my journey. Help me to study and to learn Your Word more. Bring to my mind godly friends who can give me trusted advice. Give me Your perspective to see the Father's activity around me. In all these things, build faith, confidence and patience in me as I look to You for guidance in my life. In Your powerful and wise name I pray. AMEN.

TALK TIME!

1. In what areas of life do you need guidance today? Why isn't the road always clear?
2. Before reading this lesson, what ways have you used to gain guidance in the past?
3. Review the principles involved in becoming a person after God's heart. Which ones are easier for you? Harder for you? Why?
4. Go back and look at the available tools in God's toolbox. Discuss the ways you use the Bible, other godly people, the Holy Spirit and God's activity around you to get guidance.
5. How confident do you feel in approaching God? Why?
6. Someone once said, "Lord, give me patience....and please give it now!" Is patience something tough for you? What can you learn from patience as you think about guidance?
7. Do you know someone needing guidance and direction today? How can this lesson equip you to help your friend?

6

OVERLOADED, OVERWHELMED AND TOTALLY BURNED OUT

"I am poured out like water, and all my bones are out of joint.
My heart has turned to wax; it has melted away within me.
My strength is dried up like a potsherd…"
Psalm 22:14-15a

In his book, *Laugh Again,* Chuck Swindoll admits why he is tired most of the time. I find these words hilarious.

Yes, I'm tired. For several years I've been blaming it one middle-age, iron poor blood, lack of vitamins, air pollution, saccharin, obesity, dieting, underarm odor, yellow wax build-up, and a dozen other maladies that make you wonder if life is really worth living. But now I find out, taint that. I'm tired because I'm overworked.

The population of this country is 200 million. Eighty-four million are retired. That leaves 116 million to do the work. There are 75 million in school, which leaves 41 million to do the work. Of this total, there are 22 million employed by the government. That leaves 19 million to do the work. 4 million are in the armed forces, which leaves 15 million to do the work. Take from that total the 14,800,000 people who work for the state and city governments and that leaves 200,000 to do the work. Now, there are 188,000 in hospitals, so that leaves 12,000 to do the work. Now, there are 11,998 people in prisons. That leaves just 2 people to do the work. You and me. And you're standing there reading this. No wonder I'm tired.[25]

Does this describe you? Do you feel like this at times? This type of fatigue is not necessarily physical exhaustion. All of us get tired at times from household chores, yard work or other strenuous duties. The kind of depletion I'm thinking about is the emotional and spiritual emptiness in your inner life. It's a state in your private world where you are dried up, worn out and unmotivated. You feel displaced, overwhelmed and overloaded. What's worse, you don't see any help or hope in sight. That's burnout. You're spiritually, emotionally and physically exhausted.

LESSON FOCUS

How do we get this way? What contributes to this overwhelmed state? How do you know if you're wiped out? What can you watch to help you avoid it? How can you find relief from overload? These issues and questions need careful examination and reflection in order to arrive at a sensible, realistic answer. You must look honestly at the things in your life that are causing your wick to burn low in order to see God's answers and resources to overcome it.

HOW DO YOU GET THIS WAY?

There are a number of significant diagnostic tools in the world that can help people evaluate the reasons why they run themselves into the ground these days. One such tool is the Pace of Life Index.[26] Presented as a series of 20 questions, it examines personal, daily habits to determine if a person is in a state of "high hurry," "medium hurry," or "low hurry" infirmity. For each question, three possible answers exist.

Symptomatic tools like the Pace of Life Index and others are helpful because they reveal the factors in us and around us that seek to push and to control our rate of living. Too often, we permit things

---

[25] Charles Swindoll, *Laugh Again* (Word), p. 58.

[26] Walt Schafer, *Stress, Distress and Growth* (Davis, CA. Responsible Action, Inc.1978). Also found in Injoy Life Club Lesson "Overloaded and Overwhelmed" (Atlanta: Injoy, Volume 9, #9).

and people to dictate the speed of life at which we run. When this happens, we succumb to their mandates and find ourselves sucked into a spiraling whirlpool that pulls us into a quagmire of activity and busyness that often sees no beneficial results. Take a moment now and look at the velocity of your life through this index and answer the questions honestly and thoughtfully.

The Pace of Life Index

Question	Always (3) or usually	Some-TIMES (2)	Seldom or (1) never
1. Do you find yourself rushing your speech?			
2. Do you hurry other people's speech by interrupting them with "uh-huh, hmm"or by completing their sentences for them?			
3. Do you hate to wait in line?			
4. Do you seem to be short of time to get everything done?			
5. Do you detest wasting time?			
6. Do you eat fast?			
7. Do you drive over the speed limit?			
8. Do you try to do more than one thing at a time?			
9. Do you become impatient if others do something too slowly?			
10. Do you seem to have little time to relax and enjoy the time of day?			
11. Do you find yourself over committed?			
12. Do you jiggle your knees, tap your fingers or bite your nails?			
13. Do you think about other things during conversations?			
14. Do you walk fast?			
15. Do you hate dawdling after a meal?			
16. Do you become irritable if kept waiting?			
17. Do you detest losing in sports and games?			
18. Do you find yourself with clenched fists or tight neck or jaw muscles?			
19. Does your concentration sometimes wander while you think about what's coming up later?			
20. Are you a competitive person?			

Scoring: **45-60: High hurry sickness**
35-44: Medium hurry sickness
20-34: Low hurry sickness

71

How Do You Know When You've Got It?

Any number of diagnostic tests can give a helpful snapshot of the way you respond to daily tension and pressure. But often they fail to note the distinct relationship that exists between the emotional/psychological side of a person's life to their *spiritual* life. That's where the Scriptures give us needed information to help us detect when burnout is noticeable in your inner world.

When it comes to seeing external signs that reveal internal troubles, Elijah serves as a good example. After seeing a great victory for God on Mount Carmel (I Kings 18), he flees from Queen Jezebel when he learns that his life is in danger. With fear in his heart as he comes to Beersheba, he journeys into the desert for a full day, sits under a broom tree and prays that he might die. The words, *"I have had enough, Lord. Take my life; I am no better than my ancestors"* (I Kings 19:4b) reveal a picture of an overloaded, overwhelmed and internally dried up person.

What Scriptural indicators show burnout? Obviously, one factor to consider is the *timing* of his depression. It occurred after two significant victories, recorded in 1 Kings 18. Not only was the time on Mount Carmel intense and faith-moving before the Prophets of Baal, but also the subsequent prayer to bring rain certainly secured great honor and respect for the prophet among his people during their time of drought. However, after these victories were secured, Elijah encountered a predictable down time in his inner life. He needed a retreat to gain some rest and to reflect on the way God used His power through him. But he didn't do it. He had nothing to give and it produced cracks in his life. During his time of greatest victory, Satan attacked him at his weakest point.

Another external element in the equation of Elijah's burnout is his desire to be *alone* and to wallow in *self-pity*. It's clear that he became afraid when he learned of Jezebel's intent to kill him. But there were other times when he was publicly humiliated. King Ahab insulted the prophet before Obadiah, the king's right hand man (18:17). These rejections, combined with his noticeable anger at the Prophets of Baal (18:27), the People of Israel for rejecting God (18:11) and at God Himself for drying up the brook (17:7) and for letting the widow's son die (17:20) all point to feelings of insecurity and imbalance in his personal life. He failed to ask God for strength in his inner spirit. Instead, he focused his prayers always toward other things (the dead boy, the altar sacrifice, rain, etc.) Because of this, his private chamber was undernourished and susceptible to times of intense loneliness and self-pity.

Look at his pity-party! In 1 Kings 19:14 we read, *"I have been very zealous for the Lord God Almighty. The Israelites have rejected your covenant, broken down your altars, and put your prophets to death with the sword. I am the only one left, and now they are trying to kill me too"* (my emphasis). Reading his words almost make you want to start a "gloom, despair and agony on me" gathering! But it vividly shows what fear and loneliness can do to you when you're exhausted in every area of your life. You can produce a great deal of self-pity when your attention is focused on yourself.

David gives us additional signs of burnout that a person produces during their overloaded times. In Psalm 22, you see several spiritual indicators present. *One is the feeling that God is distant.* Starting at verse 1 we read, *"My God, my God, why have you forsaken me? Why are you so far from saving me, so far from the words of my groaning? O my God, I cry out by day, but you do not answer, by night, and am not silent."* His loneliness was not only socially noticeable. It was spiritually felt too. However when he tried to call upon the Lord, he felt his prayers were bouncing off the clouds, never reaching His throne. He encountered great difficulty in finding God.

Another telltale sign coming from David's overload was his feelings of worthlessness. You see this in verse 6, *"But I am a worm and not a man, scorned by men and despised by the people. All who see me mock me; they hurl insults, shaking their heads."* Obviously, burnout compels you to exaggerate your true condition in almost every way. You're not *truly* a worm, but you *feel* like it. *Everyone* doesn't say bad things at you, but you *sense* it. When you're wiped out internally, you feel that there's nothing you can do or contribute that will make life better. These feelings of inadequacy rumble like boiling water inside you, making you think that no one really cares about your life. So you retreat and live in low esteem for a period of time.

Don't forget the *exhaustion* David felt during the process. He gives us a clear picture when he states, *"I am poured out like water, and all my bones are out of joint. My heart has turned to wax; it has melted away within me"* (Psalm 22:14-15). The fast paced demands of his life, combined with feelings of inadequacy, fear and loneliness produced a setting of spiritual drought in his inner world. Despite the fact that the Lord was his Shepherd who led David beside the still waters (one psalm later), he was currently living in a dry wasteland. He needed an oasis, but all he found was dry sand.

That's how burnout can affect your life. When you least expect it, the velocity of life can overpower you, leaving you no time to refuel and to draw strength from God. You feel it and the people around you see it. They see it in your words, your actions and most notably your attitude.

WATCHING YOUR LIFE

Scripture speaks several times to leaders about "watching your life" (1 Timothy 4:16, Acts 20:28). There are several checklist areas where you can see if overload and burnout are overwhelming your life.

Overload Checklist
- ❑ My attitude: How am I treating people at work?
- ❑ My family: How am I treating my wife? My kids?
- ❑ My devotions: Am I spending daily time with God?
- ❑ My body: How do I feel? Am I exercising daily?
- ❑ My day off: How do I spend it? What do I do?
- ❑ My tolerance level: How am I handling temptation?
- ❑ My work: Am I thinking new, creative thoughts?
- ❑ My growth: Do I want to read & to learn new things?
- ❑ My motivations: Do I want to initiate new projects?
- ❑ My time: Do I want to spend it with other people?
- ❑ My sleep: How do I wake up in the morning?
- ❑ My relationships: How do I act when the phone rings?

Picture each area like a window to the chamber of your soul. Every time you treat a subject in a negative or harmful way, it's like pulling down a dark shade on the window. When this happens, it gets darker inside. This darkness creates isolation. Before you know it, you start to feel alone and depressed, all because certain areas of your life became neglected or abused.

Generally speaking, if you can cite negative answers to four listed areas, chances are good that you are heading into a time of burnout. Five or more reveal that you are there. Six or more probably show that you're drying up and living with deep discouragement.

STOPPING BURNOUT BEFORE YOU BURN UP

All of us take on too many things at times and we pay for it eventually. But if you can learn and implement the following biblical principles, you can fight stress, overload and burnout in your daily life.

The first step is to identify the tension areas in your life right now. What brings stress to your life? Is it your family? Your work? Unresolved conflict? Unexpected crisis? Unrealistic expectations? Take some time, sit down and think. It's imperative that you discover the major sources of tension that bring frustration to your life. You can't tackle a problem without first knowing what it is. Find out what brings exhaustion and overload to your life and look at it with honesty and realism.

You may need help on this step. Talk to your spouse or to a close friend. There's a good possibility that they will bring a different perspective and outlook. Listen to their thoughts. Go through the checklist. Take a snapshot of your life and discover the diagnosis. You can't cure what you don't acknowledge.

The second step is to release the emotional garbage from your past. The Apostle Paul wrote, *"forgetting what is behind and straining toward what is ahead, I press on..."* (Philippians 3:13b). The problem with many people in burnout and overload lies in their own emotional dump truck. They have not stopped carrying bad baggage from their past. Like an anchor tied to their ankle, they drag it around heavily and painfully, not wanting to release it. Continuing to hold on, they weigh themselves with unnecessary burdens, keeping them from experiencing the freedom that comes when you cut the chains.

There is a revealing poem entitled, "The Art of Letting Go." I'd like to give credit to the author, but he/she remains unknown.

THE ART OF LETTING GO

To let go is not to care for, but to care about.
To let go is not to fix, but to be supportive.
To let go is not to judge, but to allow another
to be a human being.
To let go is not to be in the middle, arranging all the outcomes, but to allow others to affect their own destinies.
To let go is not to deny, but to accept.
To let go is not to nag, scold, or argue, but instead to search out my own shortcomings and correct them.
To let go is not to regret the past, but to grow and live for the future.
To let go is not to cut myself off. It's the realization that I can't control another.
To let go is not to try to change or blame another. It's to make the most of myself.
To let go is to fear less and to love more.

The third step in handling overload and burnout is to accept your worth before God. Like Elijah and David, when we allow the pace and pressures of life to consume us, we lose perspective and soon fall into times of intense discouragement and insecurity. When these times come, it's important to return to the Bible to see the value that God places upon us. Let these Scriptures remind you of your worth before God:

How God Values Me

- *"Therefore, there is now no condemnation for those who are in Christ Jesus"* (Romans 8:1). **Think about it—I'm no longer guilty because of Christ!**

- *"How great is the love the Father has lavished on us, that we should be called children of God! And that is what we are!* (1 John 3:1a). **Think about it—I'm deeply loved and secure in God! I'm His child!**

- *"Praise be to the God and Father of our Lord Jesus Christ! In His great mercy He has given us new birth into a living hope through the resurrection of Jesus Christ from the dead, and into an inheritance that can never perish, spoil or fade—kept in heaven for you, who through faith are shielded by God's power until the coming of the salvation that is ready to be revealed in the last time"* (1 Peter 1:3-5). **Think about it—I have a living hope and an eternal inheritance!**

- *"And why do you worry about clothes? See how the lilies of the field grow. They do not labor or spin. Yet I tell you that not even Solomon in all his splendor was dressed like one of these. If that is how God clothes the grass of the field, which is here today and tomorrow is thrown into the fire, will he not much more clothe you, O you of little faith? So do not worry, saying, 'What shall we eat?' or 'What shall we drink?' or 'What shall we wear?' For the pagans run after all these things, and your heavenly Father knows that you need them. But seek first his kingdom and his righteousness, and all these things will be given to you as well. Therefore do not worry about tomorrow, for tomorrow will worry about itself. Each day has enough trouble of its own"* (Matthew 6:28-34). **Think about it—God cares for me more than I could ever care for myself. He knows what I need! I can trust Him!**

The fourth step in handling overload and burnout is to accept your limitations before God. He has not gifted you to do everything. He has probably created and equipped you to do three or four things in life very well. Your task is to find out those strengths and to start putting priority to them. Accept the fact that you shouldn't be a "jack of all trades." Know what you do well and what you *don't* do well. Realize that you have legitimate limitations and start saying **"NO"** to the things that fall under them. You need to narrow your field. Start striking off all those things that point to your weaknesses and start delegating them to someone else.

What takes up your time and energy? Look at the things that you do at work and at home. Do you *have* to do them or are you doing them because no one else is doing them? Think about it—if no one else wants to do it and you realistically don't have to do it, it's *not* an important item. If it was significant, someone would do it! Start whittling away at the daily work list before you. What are the things that you *must* do and what are the things that others can pick up? Look around your home. What are you doing and what are your kids doing? Your children can sweep, clean bathrooms, mow the lawn, feed the animals and fix meals. Give them an opportunity!

The fifth step in handling overload and burnout is to find a confidential dumping ground. What I mean is to find someone you can talk to when you need to get some things off your chest. Everyone needs a confidential friend to bear some of life's burdens at times. James said, *"Confess your sins to each other and pray for each other so that you may be healed"* (James 5:16a). People need someone who will listen when things are bothering them. It's natural and healthy, provided you find the right person or small group. In a setting of Christian love and accountability, people need a place where they can let their hair down and get some steam off their chest. Find someone with whom you can do this. If you don't have one right this moment, you need to make a new friend and start developing a relationship with them. Don't start dumping heavy emotions on a new friend in a week! You may lose them quickly! Instead, develop a relationship that enables you to share more with them as time progresses.

One of my college professors used to tell me, "A friend will joyfully sing with you when you are on the mountaintop, and silently walk beside you through the valley." Start praying for a person right now with whom you can develop the kind of relationship that will allow you to share your troubles, hurts, burdens and tensions in life.

When you do, the words of Proverbs 17:17 will come true, *"A friend loves at all times, and a brother is born for adversity."*

The sixth step in handling overload and burnout is to feed yourself a balanced, proper diet. I'm not just thinking about food. Of course a good diet is a portion of this picture. But there must be other things besides food, work and sleep that will give you balance and well being in your life. If you only work and follow the daily grind, you'll burnout quickly. You need to find other areas to round out your life and give it completeness and perspective.

When we are overwhelmed, too often we want to close up shop and retreat into isolation. This can lead to mental and emotional shutdown. When this happens, you starve yourself spiritually, mentally, emotionally and psychologically. Find ways to invigorate and to stretch your mind. If you need a physical "pick-me-up," get some exercise and follow a nutritious diet. If you need spiritual rejuvenation, read your Bible and be sure to get to church early for worship. If your emotional life is running dull these days, by all means *take a day off* and pursue a hobby. If you find your mind is flabby and blunted, enroll in a continuing education class, buy a book tape on an interesting subject or find someone who is an expert in something you like and talk to them about it. There's no excuse when it comes to nourishing and developing your body, mind, soul and emotions. Do something different! Get out of your recliner and pursue a more balanced life!

One hobby that is therapy for me is gardening. I love working with my hands and watching things grow. Sure, gardening takes sweat and work. That's why I like it! For a person who sits behind a desk and talks to people daily on the phone, I find soil preparation, planting, cultivating and harvesting in the great outdoors so invigorating! I like to read the latest news and research in growing vegetables and flowers, so I subscribe to several quality gardening magazines. It's not a chore. It's fun! It stretches me! Likewise in your life, find something you like to do that will motivate you to grow. If you want to come into my garden and work, you're welcome!

The seventh step in handling overload and burnout is to use the Lord's Day as it was intended. Do you know why so many people are burned to the crisp on the insides these days? They haven't follow the pattern given by their Creator! If He rested one day in seven, why shouldn't we? Remember, God didn't *have* to rest after creating the universe in Genesis 1 and 2. Rather, He set the standard for us to follow. If you want to enjoy life and find fulfillment in the long haul, you'd better stop and smell the roses on the Lord's Day.

A revealing, yet often forgotten passage on the importance of the Sabbath observance is found in Isaiah 58. In eloquent form, the prophet writes:

> *"If you keep your feet from breaking the Sabbath*
> *and from doing as you please on my holy day,*
> *if you call the Sabbath a delight*
> *and the LORD's holy day honorable,*
> *and if you honor it by not going your own way*
> *and not doing as you please or speaking idle words,*
> *then you will find your joy in the LORD,*
> *and I will cause you to ride on the heights of the land*
> *and to feast on the inheritance of your father Jacob."*
> The mouth of the LORD has spoken. (58:13-14).

Observe how the prophet takes something that sounds negative and makes it positive and enriching. Too often, when the subject of the Christian Sabbath is brought up for discussion, legalistic vibrations resound. That's not God's perspective. The Lord's Day observance is not something you *have* to do; *it's something you want to do.*

Why did God design a rest day for every seven days? When you think about it, it makes sense. He intended it be a time for *rest, worship, reflection and planning.* Physically, we rest from our labors so that our bodies can recoup (Exodus 20:8-10). Spiritually, we worship with God's people to recharge our internal batteries and to get us back on track with the Lord amidst the busyness of life (Hebrews 10:25). Emotionally, we reflect on the events and circumstances of the past week, evaluating its impact upon our life (I think that's partially what the word *"Remember"* means in Exodus 20:8). Mentally, we look at the days ahead and plan our work and interests in ways that are resourceful and strategic (Psalm 37:5). I encourage you to *see the Sabbath as a positive tool to help you defeat burnout in your life. It's not intended to tie you up in legalism.*

Unfortunately, what happens too often these days? From my observations, here's why so many Christians are burned up by

Sunday night. First, they put too many things on their calendar for the week. Some of these unfinished tasks spill over into the weekend. But they can't catch up on Friday evening because that's the night of the high school football game. So it gets moved over to Saturday. But it doesn't get done then because of yard work, the kid's soccer game and their favorite college or pro team on TV that night. So they consume themselves all day Saturday in family and worldly pursuits, missing the opportunity to prepare their hearts for worship for the next day. Then they wake up late on Sunday morning and argue over whether they will go to church. Sometimes they "huff and puff" their way to worship. Other times they stay at home and try to use the day as a "catch up" time. By the time Monday morning rolls around, they have no fuel in the tank. No time was given to rest, to reflect, to worship and to plan.

I don't think I'm too far off in this assessment. People are far too tired these days. The reason is they haven't used the Lord's Day correctly. If you want to beat burnout, experience the grace and strength that can come from the Sabbath observance. God programmed it into the fabric of our life. He knew that if we didn't take time to observe it, we would grind ourselves into the ground. Go to church this Sunday and worship. Then spend some time thinking about last week, next week and what you need to do. Then talk to God about it in worship and ask Him for strength. Then take a nap and spend some time with your own family and your church family!

The eighth step in handling overload and burnout is to plan your work first, then work your plan. Planning means getting some organization into your life! Go out and buy some type of daily planner, sit down at the start of the week (that's what Sunday's for) and map out the week before you. Make sure you have all the key appointments and "to do" tasks listed in priority. Then look at each day and try to balance the tasks and appointments so that one day is not overloaded at the expense of the others. Sometimes this is challenging to do, especially if the nature of your work involves regular deadlines and presentations. However with some thought and forward planning that is bathed with prayer, you can balance your week so that you don't feel like you're working behind the proverbial eight ball of tasks, people and paperwork. The key to keeping stress from becoming distress is planning your work, *then* working your plan.

How do you plan? Jesus said in Luke 14:28, *"Suppose one of you wants to build a tower. Will he not first sit down and estimate the cost to see if he has enough money to complete it?"* While the main teaching of His analogy centers around the cost involved in discipleship, the importance of analysis and estimation can't be overlooked. Sit down today and write out all your major areas of responsibility. If you work part-time or full-time, now is a good time to pull out your job description. As you review it, say to yourself, "What are the things that I'm supposed to do each week?" Then write each responsibility on a separate 3 x 5-index card. Every week as you sit down to plan, flip through the cards and let them "jog" your memory about tasks that you need to do under each respected responsibility. For each card that strikes your mind, write down the specific task in pencil. Then schedule the task for a day on your weekly planner. It's that simple! All it takes is a little advance thought and planning. Before you know it, your productivity level will rise and you'll feel much better!

The ninth step in handling burnout and overload is to enjoy a good laugh. As I write this, you need to know that no one needs to practice this truth more than me. Like many people in the world, I get serious about too many things, failing to enjoy the moment and the day for the beauty it brings. All of us need to stop, to take a deep breath, to add some laughter to our life and to enjoy the day for a change. Do something regularly that will enliven you. Go watch a funny movie. Get with some friends and have a good time. Check out a humorous book at the library. Pull out some old family movies and have some fun. Laughter is one of the best medicines on this earth.

Joy is a choice we make. It has little to do with age, circumstances or money. It's a state of mind and heart that knows God is in control and that He will work all things out for His glory. Since He works all things together for our good (Romans 8:28), we can rest in His plan and will for our lives, enjoying His ride along the way. But it's a conscious decision every day. Will you relax and enjoy life the way God intended or will you worry and put unnecessary pressure on yourself? The choice is yours.

SUMMARY

These nine biblical steps can help any person get off to a good start in tackling the overloaded and overwhelmed areas of their life. But it takes deliberate thought and intentional action to make a change in your daily life. Are you tired of living like an emotional dump truck? Do you want to get out of the unnecessary loads and pressures that come because of forgetfulness and improper planning? Do you want to live a more balanced life? Do you want to feel more productive and enjoy life at the same time? It starts by looking at your life right now and implementing the nine steps that can balance the overloaded burdens in your life:

- ❑ **Identify the tension areas of your life.**
- ❑ **Release the emotional garbage from your past.**
- ❑ **Accept your worth before God.**
- ❑ **Accept your limitations before God.**
- ❑ **Find a confidential sounding board.**
- ❑ **Feed your life a balanced, proper diet.**
- ❑ **Use the Lord's Day as it was intended.**
- ❑ **Plan your work first, then work your plan.**
- ❑ **Enjoy a good laugh.**

What needs evaluation today?

APPLICATION

Are you overloaded and overwhelmed today? What caused it? Is the pace of your life too hectic? Do you need to slow down? Think about the past. Are you holding on to something that is wearing you down? Do you need to find a friend and to vent some frustration? How are you using the Lord's Day? Is it just another day or is it a day for rest, reflection, worship and planning? Do you take the time to plan your week? When was the last time you enjoyed a good laugh? Can you honestly accept your limitations before God? Take some time to ponder these and other issues that flow out of this chapter. Then attack the problems with God's resources and get this excessive load off your back. You'll be happier and healthier.

PRAYER

Heavenly Father, I recognize that in many respects, I've dug myself into a deep hole. I've allowed too many things and other people to dictate the pace of my life. I need You to show me my strengths and my limitations. Help me to plan properly. Today, I choose to set apart the Lord's Day for rest, worship and planning. Bring a good friend into my life who will allow me to let my hair down and share my struggles. I want to enjoy life. I'm tired of living under this pressure and intensity. Show me ways that I can live a more balanced life while staying productive in the things I'm supposed to do. Teach me to work to my strengths and to acknowledge my limitations. I want to be a more complete person. Grant this request I pray. In Jesus' Name. AMEN.

TALK TIME!

1. Think of a time you were overloaded and in burnout. What caused you to get there?
2. Take the Pace of Life Index. What did it reveal? Do others agree?
3. Review the nine biblical steps involved in watching your life. Which ones do you need to implement right away? Which one will be the most difficult? Why?
4. Do you know someone in burnout? How can this lesson equip you to help him/her?

7

IS IT TIME TO
HIT THE ROAD, JACK?

"When the uproar had ended, Paul sent for the disciples and,
after encouraging them, said good-by and
set out for Macedonia."
Acts 20:1

Jack and I had lunch the other day at our favorite barbecue joint. We ordered the usual beef brisket plate with sweet tea, found the back table by the condiment stand and sat down to eat. After I said the blessing, he looked at me and said, "Can I talk to you about something?" "Sure," I said. "What's on your mind?" From that moment, I saw and heard the pains of a frustrated young man.

Jack was a hard working, energetic youth pastor who had established a respectable ministry in a local church. However things were not progressing as he felt they should. Three hard years were invested in building this youth group from scratch. He was comforted by the times where he saw God's hand work in the lives of his students. However, some significant issues stood before him. In terms of vision, He felt the pastor and the other church leaders didn't have the same priorities in ministry that he believed were needed to take the work to the next level. In regards to accountable oversight, he felt the elders of the church weren't initiating an active leadership role in the ministry. From his perspective, the current male leadership participated in the church more like members instead of leaders. At important times in the life of the youth group where the kids and parents gathered for forum meetings, none of the elders attended, despite the fact that they knew about it.

As he talked about his frustration, Jack commented that as a whole, there were key differences in perceived priorities for involvement in the youth ministry. Although he encouraged the church officers to come to the weekly prayer meeting, he received little response from his request. He didn't sense a bond with the pastor and with the people who were assigned to work with him. He admitted that part of the blame belonged to him. There were times when he could have connected better with the pastor and the leaders. But in his defense, ministry is a two-way street. Whether it was indifference on their part or oversight on his part, he didn't feel close to several key people in the church.

Jack spent some time examining his spiritual gift-mix as it related to youth ministry. While everyone agreed that a strong teaching gift was needed, there were obvious differences after that. Jack was a good visionary and administrator; however, he perceived that the youth and the parents needed someone with strong gifts in exhortation and pastoring. He sensed an inadequacy to shepherd this part of the congregation. He was relying on others in leadership to help him with this deficiency, but few came to his aid.

Both Jack and Joyce (his wife) grew more indifferent with the community where they resided. The kind of church people that lived in this town were blue-collar factory workers. Because of their strange shift schedules, few were consistently available to meet or to help regularly. It became increasingly harder, and at times totally frustrating, to work in an environment where everything stayed up in the air from week to week. He felt that there was little stability in the ministry because too many church people were preoccupied with work, family and life itself. Jack and his wife tried to like the community and the people. But frankly, in a town with low education and lower than average wages, it was hard for them to connect. From the social graces to the manners taught to children, people acted differently, dressed differently and thought differently. Jack and Joyce felt like outsiders.

Probably one of the most glaring areas of frustration centered in their children's school. As parents, they found themselves in continual disagreement over the philosophy of teaching and the way their children should be evaluated in the classroom. When a new principal assumed office, some improvements were seen. But the same teachers stayed, continuing the monthly level. Their kids were moving into the later elementary years and they knew that a new environment was needed.

He told me that he and his wife sat down at the kitchen table to review everything a couple of days ago. As they talked, two things stood out in their mind. The first involved the feasibility of living in the town. Frankly, youth leaders receive a below average compensation. Joyce had to work out of her home as a seamstress to make ends meet. Jack's long hours kept him from taking on another part time job. With their two girls getting older, they knew life was becoming more expensive.

The second area that provoked significant discussion was the spiritual openness and parental commitment to the work. Jack was tired and frustrated from speaking to empty seats at the monthly parent's meeting. Most of the young people stated that they liked the group, but only a few invited anyone to come to church. When you looked at the congregation and the town from a spiritual point of view, you could see signs of laxity, apathy and passive antagonism. As a trained youth leader, Jack had seen other places where the Spirit of God was working. From his standpoint, he wanted to go where God's activity was plainly seen and felt. Clearly, it wasn't in this town.

He looked at me and said, "What do you think? Is it time for me and my family to move? Do we throw in the towel and shift the ministry to the leaders and the parents now? I don't know what to do." Lines of frustration etched their place on his forehead. I was looking at a defeated, lonely, burned out youth pastor who was crying out for help. What would you have told him?

AN EVERYDAY OCCURRENCE

We're living in a time where many people lose heart and hope in their work. When they reach this stage, they quit. You see it in sports where a team gives up when they know they've lost. Everyday, marriages go south when one spouse bails out on the other, thinking that quitting is the answer. You see it every hour on the job when tensions mount, regular job deadlines are missed and people in the office become unbearable. More than ever before, people want to quit. Many of them are good people like Jack. You may be one of them.

Where is God when I really need Him? Does He say anything in

His Word about this issue? When I think about quitting, are these thoughts His or mine? Is there a way I can know if He is telling me to move on to something else?

AN IMPORTANT CLARIFICATION

Before we begin an overview on this issue, it's important to understand the kind of quitting I'm talking about. Does God want me to quit being a spouse? The answer is an emphatic *NO*. Does He want me to quit my responsibilities as a parent? Again, the resounding answer is *NO*. *The issue I'm addressing in this overview is whether it's time to move on from work that was properly given to you to do something else.* Has it reached completion? Did you have the necessary resources to accomplish the task? Have you done everything in your power to make it work? What factors come to light when you review the job? Can more be done? If there is a problem, can you remedy the situation? Do you *want* to remedy it?

APPROACH TO THIS ISSUE

I know some will want me to quote a Bible verse to prove every point that is stated. But that won't happen here. I don't think you can clearly do it. The Scriptures have a lot to say about perseverance, long suffering and issues related to it. Many times these verses need to apply to the work that is given to us. At the same time, I believe there are legitimate moments when God is leading someone to a place where he knows that it's time to lay it down and to move on to a new assignment. These principles come out of an overall composite of Biblical wisdom that God gives us. This is in line with Chapter 1, section 6 of the *Westminster Confession of Faith*:

> The whole counsel of God concerning all things necessary for his own glory, man's salvation, faith and life, is either expressly set down in Scripture, or by good and necessary consequence may be deduced from Scripture.

These principles come as a result of taking the mind of God set forth in Scripture and applying these truths in daily life. As you look at this sensitive subject, understand that these principles come from a Scriptural mindset that seeks to implement the Holy Spirit's wisdom to everyday life. They can and should be evaluated and tested in your own situation.

GENERAL OBSERVATIONS—WHY DO PEOPLE QUIT?

People like my friend Jack daily wrestle with either laying aside their work or going on with perseverance. While many persist in their efforts, some decide to throw in the towel. Why? What causes people to quit?

Some people quit because of difficult people. There are those in your life that are above you, beside you and below you who can make life completely unbearable because of their attitude, work habits or views about work. Many times they are brittle and uncompromising in their positions about the things that should be done to make the work productive. Combine this with an abrasive personality and a clash is sure to happen. People's attitudes will make or break a work environment.

Robert comes to my mind when I think of difficult people. He always had to be right about everything. If I didn't take the initiative to review things with him (he was not my supervisor but an associate of mine), I would always hear from him. While his area of ministry was to pastor and to lead the junior high students, few parents wanted to talk to him because his personality was so confrontational and abrasive. He was a difficult person in every sense of the word. At times I thought that his job was to make all of us on staff feel miserable. That's what difficult people do. They make you want to quit.

Another reason why people want to quit lies in the deadlines and stresses associated with the work. People quit many times because they can't handle the pressure points of the work. There is an old saying, "If you can't take the heat, get out of the kitchen." And many do! More and more people are leaving the corporate world and starting businesses out of their home simply to relieve themselves of the pressures and demands of big company life. If you listen to them, they will say that bigger is not always better. In their mind, corporate work produces stress that turns to distress.

A third reason why people want to quit lies in purposelessness.

Many people see no value in the work they do or the relationships that come from it. They feel caught in a prison with no meaning and little direction. To them, the thought of quitting offers a release from the sense of bondage that comes from no purpose in the work.

I believe this was the biggest reason behind's Jack's dilemma in his church. From his point of view, he felt like a glorified babysitter. With little concern from the leaders to the apparent lack of interest and support from the parents, Jack sensed that he was alone in this effort. There was no teamwork in place. He felt close to no one in the church. He and his wife lived from week to week with few signs of progress in the ministry. He told me on several occasions he would return home from youth meeting with a hollow feeling inside him. He felt that he was simply passing time. Like many people, he wasn't happy with life because he wasn't happy with his work.

Another reason why people quit is because of powerlessness. Some feel like they're the only one trying to make a positive difference in the workplace, yet the ones that have the real authority are unwilling to step in and do anything. As a result, they develop a "lone ranger" mentality. Their emotional life becomes like that of Elijah when he cries out to God, *"I am the only one left."* When they need help with their specific task, no one comes with a lending hand. They're out there all alone, having no power to do anything that could bring meaningful change. To them, the lines of accountability are too narrow and constrictive. They say to themselves, "I have the responsibility, but not the authority." Because of this, many choose to hang up their cleats and to move on to something new and different. They don't want to stay under the grip of a controlling system.

There are many additional reasons why people choose to quit their jobs for something else. I've found especially with a number of professional men that many quit because of a limited perspective on their own situation. It's often true that we don't see everything that is happening around us. Sometimes we want to draw conclusions about our life, our work and our relationships without having all the information. It's important when these times come not to act in haste, but to spend careful time thinking about the landscape around us. By landscape, I'm not talking about trees and shrubs, but rather the people and the elements in your work environment that influence you. As you do this, you'll discover that there will be times when you should *not* quit. Likewise, there will also be times when you should call it quits and move on to something else. The crux of the issue lies in discernment.

WHEN YOU SHOULD **NOT** QUIT

I think that there are at least seven times when you should *not* quit. Most of them relate to the seasons of life when you're defeated regarding your work. It's better to leave when you're on the top of the mountain, not in the valley. Many people don't recognize this and they suffer the consequences for it.

When should you *not* quit? Consider these times:

1. *When you're angry, exhausted or bewildered.* The times when we are weak make us the most vulnerable to unwholesome influence. You shouldn't decide to quit something when your anger is out of control or when you can't think straight about the issues that are causing the difficulties in your life.

2. *When you're experiencing difficulty.* Just because you think that everything you're touching at the moment is breaking or going broke is not a sufficient reason for backing away from it. Everyone goes through periods when untimely actions or uninformed decisions produce costly results. Don't be singing, "Gloom, despair and agony on me" as your car pulls out of town. Even the Yankees had losing streaks in their regular season schedule.

3. *When sufficient time has not passed to look at the problem carefully.* You may think that you're the only one that cares about this job and situation, but think again. No doubt others are affected by your decision to quit. If they knew that you have spent sufficient time considering a change, the odds are strong that they would be totally surprised. Allow those around you, above you and, if necessary below you to hear the issues that surround the frustrations you have about your work. Voice them in an appropriate way at the right time so others can give you proper input and perspective.

4. *When you're living by your feelings, not by the facts.* You shouldn't

make important decisions based on "warm fuzzies." Strong facts, taken from the objective world should stay at the center of your focus. You can go far off base if you let your feelings alone guide your life. Don't live wholly in the subjective realm.

5. *When discerning people around you give credible reasons why you should stay.* They give another perspective that is valuable to the total picture. Go to a few trusted people and ask for their advice. Try to paint the picture to them in a way that is as comprehensive and honest as you can. Let them ask you questions. Be open to the counsel that they give. If they mention several things that you could do to see improvement, do them! What harm will that do?

6. *When you have unfinished objectives and goals in your current task.* If you sense that the vision you came to accomplish is not complete, chances are high that you need to step back and rethink the issue again. If there is work yet to be done, then complete it. Perhaps your friends can help you assemble a new plan of action to tackle the work with renewed vigor and zeal.

7. *When God keeps you where you are after you've initiated other opportunities.* God doesn't make mistakes with His plans for your life. If He wants you to stay in your current responsibilities, count on it. You won't leave until His sovereign hand opens the door to another opportunity. In the meantime, spend some time in the Scriptures seeking to discern what God wants you to *BE* during this time of confusion and uncertainty.

Sometimes our minds and feelings can play tricks on us as we process whether we are to stay or to leave. Deceiving circumstances and events can pop up before us, giving us some ill-conceived ideas about quitting. At times, all of us have wondered why a circumstance happened the way it did. Then we automatically conclude that God is directing us in a different way. Not necessarily! When you come to those times, you need some solid check points along the way that will help ground you and give you sanity in the process.

CHECKPOINTS TO ACKNOWLEDGE WHEN YOU'RE TEMPTED TO THROW IN THE TOWEL

The following biblical thoughts and themes have greatly helped me during the times when I sensed that I was moving into a transition time in my life and work.

- Checkpoint #1: *MY CALL.* I must reaffirm my calling from God. I know He has me here for a reason. I am to stay true to the passion God gave me. The Father called me to serve. The Son commissioned me to be one of His followers. The Spirit has empowered me to do God's will. Major on the majors and minor on the minors.
- Checkpoint #2: *MY LIFE.* My life is not my own. I belong to someone. Not only do I belong to God, but also to my wife and to my children. I have a responsibility to God for them. This is not just about me.
- Checkpoint #3: *MY ROLE.* I know that life isn't easy right now. In fact, it's a struggle. But my role right now is to persevere and to obey God anyway. Faithfulness to God at this point is taking the resources that He *has* given me and doing the best I can to yield the greatest fruit with all the strength I can muster.
- Checkpoint #4: *MY BRAIN.* God has given me a mind to think and a heart to discern. What does He want me to learn from this situation at this time? Am I watching and learning everything that I need to know right now?
- Checkpoint #5: *MY ATTITUDE.* What is my mood toward my work? How do I act toward my spouse and children? Is my struggle affecting them? Can others detect a suspicious spirit in my life?
- Checkpoint #6: *MY FRIENDS.* Can they offer any help and insight to me right now? Do I need to sit down and to talk to them about my situation? God gives me other people to sharpen me. Am I using them?

When you start discerning these checkpoints, you can gain some valuable perspective. You'll see that at certain times, you should *not* quit. But there will also come times when you know that it's time to close the chapter on this book and to move on to new pages in your life. But how can you discern when it's the right time? When will you know that it's time to leave?

WHEN IT'S TIME TO QUIT[27]

I can think of at least seven times when you can receive some peace of mind and heart about moving on to another job or ministry. You can rest on these sensible principles when it comes to discerning a call or a job change.

1. *When others confirm that God is calling you away.* Many times God puts opportunities in front of you that capitalize on your past experiences, education and convictions. Then He sends a spirit of unrest within you, sometimes suddenly or over a period of time that tells you to look at this opportunity more carefully. If you sense through prayer and through the trusted advice of other friends who know you and your current job that the proposed opportunity is suited for you, your family and the situation as a whole, then possibly it's time to move. In most cases, God uses *people* to confirm His plans and purposes. The key is watching His activity, listening to your heart as He speaks to you, submitting to His will and hearing the confirmation from others who know you and the situation well enough.

2. *When you sense completion and peace of accomplishment in your present work.* Even Jesus said, *"It is finished"* on the cross (John 19:30). He completed the work His Father gave Him to do. In a similar way, there will come times in the seasons of your life when you realize that you have accomplished what you set out to do with a particular job. The goals and objectives have been

---

[27] Some of the thoughts from this section came from John Maxwell's Injoy Life Lessons "When to Move in Leadership" and "When to Quit." The Injoy Group, Inc. P.O. Box 7700 Atlanta, GA 30357-0700.

clearly stated and fulfilled to the best of your ability. When you sense closure, it's possible that it's time to move on and to do something else. It may simply mean a transfer to another department or a new opening in another branch of the company. It could also mean a complete change and uprooting to something completely different. Completion is only one side of the coin. It states you're done. But it can't tell you about the other side. It can only release you to look into the future.

3. *When others recognize that your abilities and talents have matured you beyond the current task.* In many instances, your current responsibilities give you wisdom and abilities that can prepare you for another level once you've learned and implemented them. But the key is that *others* recognize this. Don't go on a self-promotion tour in your office or work site. Let others see the progress and maturity in your life. Let them acknowledge that it's time for you to go elsewhere. In fact, if you do it right, they will be your biggest promoters and best references on your résumé.

4. *When things are going well, not poorly.* I've seen people leave under duress and difficulty when they should have stayed in the situation and tried to fix the problems associated with the work. There are exceptions to this general principle, but as a basic rule of thumb, try to leave a job on good grounds with your parishioners, colleagues and supervisors. Remember this—you never know when you may have to go back and use someone in your past for help in the future. Generally speaking, you *burn* bridges when you leave on bad times and you *build* bridges in good times. Leave when things are going well. If you do, people will kiss you, not spit at you.

5. *When the harvest from your labors is all in the storage bins.* The farmer never finishes his work for the growing season until all of the grain has been harvested. Likewise, it's possible that when you get to a place where all the fruit has ripened and matured, you need to assess your situation after the harvest. Do you need to start plowing again? Should you continue in this field and start

the sowing process again? Or, should you find another field in which to work? Examine the crop that has come from the labors of your mind and hands. Evaluate the things you've learned from this work experience over the years and discern your stage in the process. Are you sowing? Cultivating? Fertilizing? Harvesting? The stage you're in will likely help you discern what you need to do next.

6. *When God comes knocking on your door and you know it.* Sometimes, things are so clear from His hand that it can be downright *scary*. If you sense that He is in this opportunity (you'll know it), move toward it with faith and confidence. If He doesn't want you in it, He'll let you know in a number of ways. But when you see the opportunity coming, don't think about the benefits, perks or compensation associated with the new opening. Ask yourself and others close to you, *"Is God in it? Do I see His Hand in this opportunity?"*

7. *When you sense peace of heart about leaving your old work behind.* Pray about your present situation. Ask God to show you if your current work is really complete. Do you feel you've stayed long enough to see some accomplishments? There's nothing scientific about this, but I've learned from experience and from the counsel of others that you need at least three years to come to any conclusion about this. Do you feel good about your work today? If you had a choice to stay, would you be willing? On the other hand, do you sense excitement about this new opportunity or restlessness about your current tasks? The issue revolves around your own peace of heart and *your family's peace of mind* where applicable. If your spouse has an inner security about leaving and going to a new challenge, that's generally a positive step. With children, listen to their concerns and do all you can to provide stability for them in this timeframe. But don't base your total decision to move on whether they approve of it or not. Children adapt much faster to new friends and new environments than adults do.

While most of these principles deal with positive experiences in the workplace, there are negative times when a person's values, goals or philosophy of work or ministry clash with the mindset or direction of the company or church leaders. My friend Jack had this happen to him. He realized after doing everything he could that the leaders of his church didn't agree with his direction and actions in youth ministry. He tried to do everything to make it work, but in the end they didn't share his vision. So with a clear conscience, he stepped away from it. He was already frustrated and didn't want to dig a deeper hole. Besides, he realized that a person with a different gift-mix and temperament was needed to deal with the youth and their families. In a sense, he felt that this "plateaued" state was designed by God to show him the full picture of his work. When he saw it, he knew that he had done everything he could do in the work. He was faithful with the resources God gave him. The youth group grew during his time. Lives were changed. Fruit was seen. But the time came for him to leave. He felt uneasy at the start, but grew more satisfied with the decision as the days went by. If this situation confronts you, do all you can to rectify the issues. Work hard at creating stability so that progress can come. But if you've done everything you can with peace of mind and heart, move on to other fields. Don't let others keep you from fulfilling the convictions God gave you.

These principles can give you objective, rational reasons for deciding whether it's time to move. Often the problems become too foggy and unsettling as we look at all the factors associated with a move in our work. So remember the value of others in the process of discernment. Has all the fruit been picked? Have you matured beyond this level? Do you have peace of mind and heart about leaving? Is God knocking? Do others see it? Let the Holy Spirit speak to you and to others as you proceed with the evaluation process.

CAN YOU KNOW FOR SURE IF YOU MADE THE RIGHT DECISION?

My friend Jack chose to leave the work at the church and to pursue a job in the marketplace with his cousin selling and installing swimming pools. To my knowledge, it's turned out to be a good move for him. He likes his new work and makes a comfortable living. He's also become active as a deacon in his new church, serving as the chairman of the Youth Activities Committee. He's been an invaluable help to the current youth director in many ways. He gave this youth director something he didn't have when he was in that position. God sovereignly prepared Jack to minister and to mentor this new youth pastor in a growing ministry. It's been a win-win situation everywhere.

Even though it looks good now, I'm sure the first couple of months in his new work caused Jack to ask some reflection questions. Did I make the right decision? Am I at peace with myself? How can I know that I did the right thing? Several things stand out that can help him and others who face this dilemma.

1. *You know it's right if the task left behind stays ongoing and keeps on progressing.* John Maxwell said it well, "There is no success without a successor." Part of leaving a job or ministry well is to do everything possible to see that the work continues going on in a good direction. This means several things. On the one hand, it means training the people to handle the ministry until a new leader is found. On the other hand, it also means securing the necessary resources in order to take that job through the transition time. When you look back and see that the old work is doing fine, chances are good that you left it at the right time.

2. *You know it's right when you experience God's blessing on your new work.* After all, if you were led to this new vineyard by God's hand, it stands to reason that He picked you to work it so that His glory would be seen in it, producing a blessing for all to see. Look for clear signs of God's fruit in your current work. You can tell that if you talk more about your current work than you talk about your old work, chances are good that you've been transplanted properly and that you're bearing fruit in good season.

3. *You know it's right when your family is settled and comes to peace with the move.* So often, they look at the tangibles associated with moving. What kind of house will we get? Will I make any new friends? What kind of neighborhood will we find? Can we identify with the people? How are the schools? Can we afford to live here and enjoy it? These and other questions like it need

to be asked regularly and often during the first few months of the transition. Generally speaking, if positives come out of this evaluation and your family is satisfied, you made the right decision at the right time.

4. *When you can't go back.* If you've grown and developed to the point where you can't return to your old job, you're probably at the right place. How do you know? When you look back and see how God used your gifts and abilities in your old work at that time, but those things aren't needed there now. When the hearts of the people in your former place have changed allegiance to the person that followed you, you know you can't go back. You made the right choice to leave when you did. This can be an emotional challenge to accept this at times, but it's reality. God uses us at certain times in certain places as a part of His sovereign plan. Going back would be like the Israelites going back to Egypt. It can't be done. You're different. They're different. You can go back to visit upon an invitation, but don't stay. Look ahead and not back.

SUMMARY

We've had an opportunity to learn why people often quit. Sometimes they leave for the wrong reasons. Other times, they quit for positive reasons. We've examined the times *NOT* to quit as well as the times when the writing on the wall says, "You need to leave." Keep in mind the checkpoints in the process along the way. Remember your calling from God as you look at your life and role. Your life doesn't belong to you. It belongs to Christ. He has a sovereign plan for your life to prosper you and to give you hope and a future (Jeremiah 33:11). *God calls you TO things, not FROM things.* Even Abraham was called to leave so that he could go to something better. Keep your attitude in check and wait upon the Lord to give you wisdom through friends and family. They can give you guidance and perspective as you move step by step in the process. And through it all, ask God to give you a peace no matter what happens. With God in your corner, nothing can stop you from doing the right thing.

APPLICATION

Is this a tension point in your life right now? Are things going well or sour in your current work? If things are not well, are you trying to change them? What are you specifically trying to do? Are others cooperating with you or are they nominally uninvolved? Can you say that you've tried or done *everything* you could possibly do? Is the harvest from your labors complete? What about other opportunities? Are they on the horizon? Is God's activity in it? Are people coming to you or are you going to them? Are others around you, especially your spouse, telling you that it's time to move? Do you have a peace of mind about going? If you do, are you taking the necessary steps to insure a good transition. Remember, there is no success without a successor. Let God show Himself to you during this stage of your life as you wait upon Him to lead you step by step. Sometimes the road isn't clear, but in the long run, the journey is rewarding.

PRAYER

Let the following prayer by Thomas à Kempis (1380-1471) give you perspective and help as you discern this important transition in your life:

> Grant me, O Lord, to know what I ought to know,
> To love what I ought to love,
> To praise what delights Thee most,
> To value what is precious in Thy sight,
> To hate what is offensive to Thee.
>
> Do not suffer me to judge according to the sight
>   of my eyes,
> Nor to pass sentence according to the hearing of the ears
>   of ignorant men;
> But to discern with a true judgment between things
>   visible and spiritual,
> And above all, always to inquire what is the good pleasure
>   of Thy will. Amen.

TALK TIME!

1. Are you thinking about quitting right now? What are your reasons? Are they valid?
2. Review the reasons listed when quitting should *NOT* be considered. Do any of these strike close to home for you?
3. What are other discerning people saying about all this in your life? Have you talked to them? Are they aware of your situation?
4. Go over the checkpoints listed when you think about throwing in the towel. Do any of them bring comfort?
5. Have you ever been in a situation where you knew God was knocking with an opportunity? Describe it with as many specifics as you can.
6. How important is it to leave when things are going well? Is this really important?
7. Discuss the principles that will help you know if you've made the right decision. Is this really significant?
8. Do you know someone who is thinking about quitting? How can this lesson equip you to help them? How can you be a good friend to someone else as they seek advice whether they should make a change in their life?

8

DON'T JUST DO SOMETHING—
STAND THERE!

"The Lord will fight for you; you need only to be still."
Exodus 14:14

It was less than forty-eight hours away and nothing looked promising. My close friend Joe, a respected and popular local judge, and I had formed a private foundation to send deserving young people from the area's public housing communities to a state university on a fully funded, four-year scholarship that included tuition, books, room and board. The scholarship recipient came from the housing neighborhood that documented the most progress in improving their community life over the year. At the end of December, they turned in their scrapbooks to an independent panel to determine the winner. The Riverside Heights community won the competition and nominated a graduating senior named Cheryl to receive the "Operation Pride" scholarship. Excitement ran high in the neighborhood, as a major press conference was less than two days away. Newspapers, television and radio reporters notified us that they were coming. Everything fell in place except one thing. *We didn't have the money.* We needed $5,000 immediately to give to the official representing Cheryl's future school. Joe and I were starting to sweat. We didn't know what to do and the clock was ticking.

All kinds of thoughts ran through my mind. If nothing happens, what do we tell everyone at the press conference? What will this mean to the winning housing community? How will Cheryl and her family feel? With these and many other emotions, Joe and I cried out to the Lord and asked Him to provide. We waited another night and still no sign surfaced. With one day and counting, we became afraid.

The next morning, Joe was in court, so we didn't talk to one another until noon. Still no word came from anyone as we got a bite of lunch. However when both of us went back to our offices, Joe noticed that a message was waiting for him from the office of a prominent businessman in town. His newly hired assistant called and asked him to call him back.

"Judge, I'm Rudy, Mr. Johnson's new administrative assistant. I'm going through a few pending files and I noticed this request that you and a Pastor McDaniel sent us about a scholarship. Is this still valid?"

"Why, yes it is."

"I'm glad to hear this. I believe this is something Mr. Johnson would be interested in doing. When do you plan to award the scholarship?"

"Tomorrow."

"Tomorrow! I'd better get busy on this. Will you be near your phone within the next hour?" I'll go talk to Mr. Johnson right now."

"Sure, I'll be here."

Less than twenty minutes went by before Rudy called Joe's office. "Mr. Johnson will be glad to fund this scholarship. We'll be there tomorrow at noon *with the check and the plaque*."

Joe could hardly contain himself when he called me. "You better sit down and hear today's divine appointment," he said. When he shared the news, we both laughed and cried over the phone. We knew God had led us to start this foundation, but we didn't know how it would be funded initially. In the midst of our fear, He broke through with the fulfillment of His promise. I've never forgotten that lesson. I learned from that experience and others since then that *in the midst of fear, don't just do something—stand there and watch God work!*

There is an old Indian fable about a mouse that was in constant distress because of its fear of the cat. A magician took pity on it and turned the mouse into a cat. Immediately, this new cat became afraid of the dog. So the magician turned it into a dog. Immediately, this new dog began to fear the tiger. So the magician turned it into a tiger. Immediately, this new tiger began to fear the hunter. With all these changes and no progress, the magician said,

"Be a mouse again. You have only the heart of a mouse and I can't help you."

I'm not going to ask you if you're afraid today. *I know you are.* Each of us has fears of living and fears of dying. When certain times of panic come, we ask ourselves many questions. And if you're like me, you were instilled with a famous cartoon line that was supposed to help in times of fear and tension:

DON'T JUST STAND THERE—DO SOMETHING!

Somehow, many of us got the idea that if we were afraid, we just needed to do something about it. You know, "work it out." However, the more I understand the way God operates, the more I'm beginning to see that this is not the way He wants us to respond when times of crisis and tension come our way. If there's anything I see, *it's just the opposite.* In times of fear and uncertainty, God doesn't want me to do anything! He wants me to stand there and watch Him work out all things according to His own glory! This lesson is clearly seen in Moses' life from Exodus 14.

LESSON FOCUS

When we encounter times of fear and crisis in our lives, God promises to work for us not only by fighting and defeating His and our enemies, but also by giving us true and precious promises that can help us experience His greatness and glory on a higher level. Exodus 14 is an account of *stillness before the Lord*, something busy, high-energy people like me and others need to practice if we're to know God more intimately.

BAITING THE HOOK FOR THE ENEMY

Through God's power, Moses performed many miraculous wonders and plagues upon Egypt. After each plague, Pharaoh's heart hardened. He determined to keep the Israelites in slavery. Finally through the death of the first born (Exodus 11-12), the King of Egypt freed them to go and to worship the God of their fathers. God guided them through the wilderness with a pillar of cloud during the

day and a pillar of fire by night (Exodus 13:21-22). The Children of
Israel knew God was guiding and leading them to a new home.

With this as a background, there's something powerful to understand in Exodus 14:2 that most people don't pick up with a casual
reading. God tells Moses, *"Tell the Israelites to **turn back** and
encamp near Pi Hahiroth, between Migdol and the sea"* (my
emphasis). Moses and the people were headed for the Promise
Land, but God tells them *to turn around*. Respected commentators
C.F. Keil and F. Delitzsch affirm this in their scholarly analysis:

> If Israel therefore did not go straight into the desert from
> Etham, on the border of the desert, but went southwards
> into the plain of Suez, to the west of the head of the Red
> Sea, they were obliged to bend round, *i.e.* "to turn" from
> the road they had taken first…This turn in their route was
> not out of the way for the passage through the Red Sea;
> but apart from this, it was not only out of the way, but a
> very foolish way, according to human judgment. God
> commanded Moses to take this road, that He might be
> honoured upon Pharaoh, and show the Egyptians that He
> was Jehovah.[28]

What's happening at this point is extraordinary. *God is preparing
to teach the Israelites a powerful lesson by using them as bait.* God
dangles them like the latest fishing lure before the Egyptian army
and stimulates Pharaoh to pursue them like a hungry large mouth
bass. In other words, *this is a divine setup.* God engineered a crisis
to teach the Children of Israel a lesson about stillness.

When the Israelites looked up, they saw Pharaoh and his army
charging after them. Exodus 14:10 says, *"they were terrified and
cried out to the Lord."* They didn't know what to do! They were
slaves! The only thing they knew to do was manual labor! They
weren't trained to fight like an army! Most likely they said to themselves, *"We're doomed for sure! We can't stand up against the
Egyptians! They are a well-oiled machine!"*

[28] C.F. Keil and F. Delitzsch, *Commentary on the Old Testament*, Volume 2 of the Penta-
teuch, p. 43.

WE'RE NO DIFFERENT

We think like that at times. We panic when we see trouble marching our way. We live with too much fear, wondering how we're going to handle a forthcoming problem. The Israelites thought that the end was near. We say that sometimes too. Why? What causes us to fear so many things?

One reason we fear is because of personal comfort. Notice the response of the Israelites to Moses in Exodus 14:11, *"Was it because there were no graves in Egypt that you brought us to the desert to die? What have you done to us by bringing us out of Egypt?"* Listen to their cries. In their minds, this would never have happened if they had stayed in Egypt. They could have lived in comfort—slavery for sure, but a *comfortable slavery.* Many of them didn't want to step out and to experience the freedom God wanted them to have in the Promised Land. They wanted to stay in their own comfort zone, even if it meant slavery. That's one reason we panic. We know our comfort zone is threatened. There was nothing they could do to stop Pharaoh's forces from coming. All they could do was stand, watch and fear.

Another reason we fear is because of personal peace. This is a kissing cousin to the previous reason but it deserves its own spotlight. In Exodus 14:12 we read, *"Didn't we say to you in Egypt, 'Leave us alone; let us serve the Egyptians? It would have been better for us to serve the Egyptians than to die in the desert!"* Again, notice their thinking. They're saying, "Leave us alone." In other words, I don't want to be bothered. I'm in my own world. As long as it doesn't affect me, that's ok. When they were in Egypt, things were in their control. Yes, taskmasters dominated their life, but they *could* control their own work. Life was predictable for them. But now, out in the desert, it's out of their control. This brought fear, panic and insecurity to their mind. They had been in control up to this point. Now they were discovering that someone was pulling the rug out from under them.

At this point, those who allow their personalities and insecurities to get in the way start scrambling. They say to themselves, "OK, something's got to happen. We need to do something about this! Don't just stand there, do something! Get busy! Think of a solution!" I can say this with full confidence, because *I've been there and done that*! It's at this point that we need to understand something. If the enemy is advancing toward you, don't do anything! *God wants you to stand there and watch Him do the work*!

A FRONT ROW SEAT

It's easy to imagine the fears of the people at this point, *but not the intensity of their feelings*. They were in mortal terror. They were trapped and could go nowhere. The Red Sea was behind them and a powerful army was coming straight toward them. For all they knew, death was coming right at them. What would you do in this situation? If you're like me, you'd give your best possession to find a way to escape. *But that didn't happen*. Look at Moses' words to the people while they were trembling with fear. He says, *"Do not be afraid. Stand firm and you will see the deliverance the Lord will bring you today. The Egyptians you see today you will never see again."* What happened was almost too incredible to believe. God put them on the fifty-yard line as witnesses to a large-scale event unparalleled in its day. He was going to win a great contest and they would be His spectators in the stands. And they didn't need a ticket.

Let this sink in. They were told *not to do anything*! Instead, they were instructed to stand still and to see the salvation of the Lord. Their human efforts would not bring them deliverance at that point. They had to wait upon God to experience full and final deliverance from the Egyptians. This is a lesson that is just as true for us as it was for the Children of Israel. *DON'T DO ANYTHING. JUST STAND STILL.* Watch what God can do when a group of people come to the place in their life where they know that if God's not in it, it's doomed to failure. That's the kind of life God wants us to live. It's life on the cutting edge. It's a life of faith and adventure. It's a life of dependence and reliance upon God. It's where God wants you to be today because when you put yourself in this type of situation, God wants to show many promises about Himself to those who stop, look and wait.

PROMISES YOU CAN TAKE TO THE BANK

Can you see something coming toward you today that is bringing fear into your life? Are you uneasy about this transitional stage of your life? Take heart! There are some powerful promises that God wants to give you! In fact, He may do it the same way that He did for the Israelites, just to get your undivided attention. What does He want you to see?

God's first promise to us is that He goes before you and behind you. In Exodus 14:19 we read, *"Then the angel of God, who had been traveling in front of Israel's army, withdrew and went behind them. The pillar of cloud also moved from in front and stood behind them."* Obviously this is a picture of protection, but it could also portray something else. While Moses stretched forth his hands to witness God's parting of the waters, God's angel is in a perfect position *to push* the Children of Israel into the floor of the Red Sea when the land became walkable. Chances are good that even if the Israelites saw the pathway before them, they *wouldn't* have moved forward unless Moses led them from the front and God pushed them from the back. In a sense, you could say that the Red Sea represented their future, yet they were unsure about stepping into it. Likewise, a figurative Red Sea stands before us at times and we don't want to step forward. That's when God comes and pushes us. Sometimes in all our uncertainty about the future, it's comforting to know that God is behind us all the way!

Too many people worry about their future. Whether it's their job, their health, their children, their finances or a host of other things, they oftentimes lose the confidence they need to live each day knowing that God is behind them. Dick Sheppard (1880-1937), renowned chaplain at Oxford House once said, "If you fear for the future, remember that the future is not likely to be half as bad as you think, and that if evils do come hurling down upon you there is being prepared for you now just the strength that you will need to confront them."[29] The man that wrote these words knew that God's

---

[29] Dick Shepherd, "Meeting Troubles Half-Way" sermon from *Christian World Pulpit* (London: May 7, 1931) in *Twenty Centuries of Great Preaching* (Word, 1971), Volume 9, p. 158.

strength was with him because poor health dominated most of his adult life.

God's second promise to us is that He fights for you in the conflict. In Exodus 14:14, Moses told the people, *"The Lord will fight for you; you need only to be still."* Israel's leader understood something we need to realize as we look at fear's approaching charge. *These are God's battles.* God is working out His good and perfect plan in us and we get the opportunity to see it up close. And because this view is only a stone's throw away, we get to see the Lord in a way we don't normally see Him in the comfort zone. We see Him going to battle for us.

I can only imagine the power of the song that Moses and the people sang in the next chapter. The people understood that God fought the battle and won for His glory. There must have been some kind of good party when they celebrated God's victory in battle.

> *I will sing to the Lord, for He is highly exalted. The horse and the rider He has hurled into the sea. The Lord is my strength and my song; He has become my salvation. He is my God, and I will praise Him, my father's God, and I will exalt Him. The Lord is a warrior; the Lord is His name. Pharaoh's chariots and His army He has hurled into the sea* (Exodus 15:1-4).

We need to see that the conflicts and skirmishes of our lives are not our battles. They are God's opportunities to show Himself strong and powerful in the affairs of our life.

God's third promise to us is that He will confound the enemy. Look at the way the Egyptian army recognized God's activity in Exodus 14:23, *"The Egyptians pursued them, and all Pharaoh's horses and chariots and horsemen followed them into the sea. During the last watch of the night the Lord looked down from the pillar of fire and cloud at the Egyptian army and threw it into confusion. He made the wheels of their chariots come off so that they had difficulty driving. And the Egyptians said, 'Let's get away from the Israelites! The Lord is fighting for them against Egypt.'"*

What a sight to see! When God is doing His work, you can see things happen! In this account, He went against the forces of evil which were trying to defeat Israel and take her back into bondage. But

He said to them, "No more! You're finished!" He caused so much confusion that they couldn't accomplish their goal. Even the enemy knew that God was at work! There was no doubt from any side as to who was in charge! In minutes, God did what no one else could do. Likewise in your life, God can supernaturally change everything in front of you by His might so that you can see His power at work. Is He making it hard for your enemies to drive on your turf?

God's fourth promise to us know is that He defeats the enemy. A vivid picture appears in Exodus 14:26, *"Then the Lord said to Moses, 'Stretch out your hand over the sea so that the waters may flow back over the Egyptians and their chariots and horsemen.' Moses stretched out his hand over the sea, and at daybreak the sea went back to its place. The Egyptians were fleeing toward it, and the Lord swept them into the sea. The water flowed back and covered the chariots and horsemen—the entire army of Pharaoh that had followed the Israelites into the sea. Not one of them survived. But the Israelites went through the sea on dry ground, with a wall of water on their right and on their left. That day the Lord saved Israel from the hands of the Egyptians, and Israel saw the Egyptians lying dead on the shore."*

The picture conveyed in this description is that the Egyptian army tried to flee the forthcoming judgment from the Lord, but could not escape. In a true sense, they attempted to run away from the sovereignly produced tidal waves, *but God sucked them back into the sea.* That's where the phrase "the Lord swept them into the sea" comes in. It's more than bad timing on the Egyptians' part. *God* engineered this action so that Israel saw the outcome. He wanted them to see up close and first hand *how* He would defeat their enemies if they would stand still and watch with prayerful dependence. In a similar way, God wants us to trust Him when our enemies advance against us. He's telling us the same thing Moses told the people—*"The Lord will fight for you; you need only to be still."* When you're still, God has your attention and can show you the way He wants to gain the victory in your life over your enemies!

It's interesting in passing to see how this judgment of water parallels the judgment that God used upon the world in Noah's time. While His people were protected and secure, His enemies experienced the defeat of their life. Just as Noah and his family worshipped God with a sacrifice when they got off the ark, so Moses and the people worshipped the Lord with songs of incredible celebration in Exodus 15. Both situations showed God's initiative and victory in a crisis time. Likewise for us, we can experience the realness of His promises when we stand still and watch Him work.

LESSONS FROM THE OBSERVATION TOWER

Are you pinned in a corner today? Is the battle coming to you? Do you find yourself trapped in a fearful situation? God may be saying to you, *"Don't just do something—STAND there!"* Watch and see His activity from this experience. You never know—He may be opening a Red Sea before you!

But you may be asking, "Why?" Why would God put me through this? Why does He want me to experience this kind of crisis? What is there to learn from situations like this in my life?

God uses these occasions to teach us valuable lessons about ourselves and about Him as we watch Him work from our observation tower. Throughout the Book of Exodus, you constantly see how God hardened Pharaoh's heart so that he would eventually pursue Israel. Continually, God uses the pronoun "I" to teach Moses what He is going to do. This was nothing short of a dramatic teaching lesson. And it wasn't simulated! God used real life players instead of toys. This course was entitled, "Life with God on the Cutting Edge: 101." And when God does the teaching, He brings His own visual aids. He used the Egyptians as His instruments to teach His people several valuable lessons that we can apply in our lives.

One clear lesson is His greatness. You see this several times in Exodus 14. In verse 4 we read, *"And I will harden Pharaoh's heart, and he will pursue them. **But I will gain glory for myself** through Pharaoh and all his army, and the Egyptians will know that I am the Lord."* In verse 18 we read, *"The Egyptians will know that I am the Lord **when I gain glory** through Pharaoh, his chariots and his horsemen."* And in verse 31 we read, *"And when the Israelites saw **the great power the Lord displayed** against the Egyptians, the people feared the Lord and put their trust in Him and in Moses his servant"* (my emphasis). God supernaturally engineered this entire event so that the people would see His greatness up close. He's so great, yet

He wants to be so intimate! *He wanted them to see His greatness just a few feet away.* He wanted to display His omnipotence at a private viewing. And His people got the only preview showing! Oh, how great and intimate is His power to those who believe!

Fanny Crosby said it well:

> Safe in the arms of Jesus, Safe on His gentle breast,
> There by His love o'er shadowed, Sweetly my soul
>   shall rest.
> Hark! 'tis the voice of angels, Borne in a song to me,
> Over the fields of glory, Over the Jasper sea.
> Safe in the arms of Jesus, Safe on His gentle breast,
> There by His love o'er shadowed, Sweetly my soul
>   shall rest.[30]

God engineers many of your crisis times so that in the midst of your bewilderment and helplessness, you will see His power first hand. Let Him do the work and while this is going on, rest in the security of His intimacy.

Another clear lesson we can learn is in the testimony God wants to make through us to the world. God's glory is the testimony to the world of His sovereign witness and monarchial rule. Throughout Exodus, you see the phrase, *"I will gain glory"* a number of times. In 14:17 we read, *"And I will gain glory through Pharaoh and all his army, through his chariots and his horsemen. The Egyptians will know that I am the Lord when I gain glory through Pharaoh, his chariots and his horsemen."* Like the Israelites, we need to remember that God brings these times of fearful crisis in our lives so that He can shine! It's profound but true—He chooses people like you and me as entry points to show His incredible eminence to the world. Why He wants to pick people to display His wonders is a mystery to me, but that shows how great a God He really is! He wants to shine through you to the people in your world!

A few nights ago as my wife and I were taking our normal evening exercise walk with our dog in the neighborhood, both of us commented that the moon was abnormally bright; so bright that it

---

[30] Fanny Crosby, "Safe in the Arms of Jesus" in *The Presbyterian Hymnal* (Richmond, 1949), #207.

illuminated the street before us remarkably. You could hardly look up because it was so bright! Then a simple thought hit me. The moon isn't generating any light on its own. It's purely *reflecting* what is given it from the sun. We're like that with regards to our relationship to Christ. The Lord wants us to absorb His incredible grace and love in such a way that our life radiates the light of the gospel to the people around us. And sometimes the best times that people can see it are the crisis times. These window periods perk people's attention. They cause others to look at you. No doubt some of them think, "How does a professing Christian handle this situation in their life?" Because of God's providence, you're placed in this position to testify about His character. How will you respond? Will you shine or will you sulk?

Another significant lesson that God wants us to learn from crisis is the importance of stillness before the Lord. In fact, I believe that's the major lesson conveyed in Exodus 14. Moses told the people in verse 14, *"The Lord will fight for you; you need only to be still."* Psalm 46:10a says, *"Be still, and know that I am God."* The simple truth is that you can't know God if you're too busy. You can't experience His deliverance if *you're* the one who's trying to fight all the battles of your life. You can't see His footprints if you call on Him when *you* want to have Him. Those that journey through the valley of crisis understand the value of stillness before the Lord. They wait. They pray. They meditate. They pause to watch the direction of His activity around them. Then they follow His trail.

Speaking straight from experience, it's hard to be still. It means patience, faith, quietness, peace and a realization that God, not me, is in charge of things. J. D Smith said it best when he penned this great poem about the process and value of waiting upon God. There are some great lessons in these lines. Don't skip over them quickly.

> Waiting! Yes, patiently waiting!
> Till next steps made plain shall be;
> To hear, with the inner hearing,
> The Voice that will call for me.
>
> Waiting! Yes, quietly waiting!
> No need for an anxious dread;
> Shall He not assuredly guide me,

Who giveth me daily bread?

Waiting! Yes hopefully waiting!
With hope that needn't grow dim;
The Master is pledged to guide me,
And my eyes are unto Him.

Waiting! Yes expectantly waiting!
Perhaps it may be today
The Master will quickly open
The gate to my future way.

Waiting! Yes trustfully waiting!
I know, though I've waited long,
That, while He withholds His purpose,
His waiting cannot be wrong.

Waiting! Yes waiting, still waiting!
The Master will not be late;
He knoweth that I am waiting
For Him to unlatch the gate.[31]

SUMMARY

As we've looked at Moses and the Israelites in Exodus 14, we've seen that we're no different from them when it comes to crisis. But God engineers these times to teach us some valuable promises and lessons about life. We've seen that our fear comes from wanting to stay in our personal comfort zones where there's peace and safety. However, God doesn't want us to stay in the nest. He wants us to look up and watch Him work during our times of crisis and transition. He has some incredible assurances to teach us as we sit on the front row of His sovereign cinema. But we'll never learn these promises about His greatness, His glory and His victory unless we choose to be still and let Him fight the battles for us. When crisis and fear come, *don't do anything—just stand there!* You'll be amazed when you see the new roads that He will open for you!

---

[31] Poem found in *Encyclopedia of 7700 Illustrations* (Assurance Publishers, 1979), p. 1567.

APPLICATION

Do you see transition and crisis coming toward you? If you do, how easy or difficult is it to remain still? Is it hard for you to wait? For me, it isn't pleasant! It makes me squirm and scramble for security and stability. How about you? Do you stay in your comfort zone? Are you tempted to try to do something just to gain some kind of emotional control? Are you seeing now from this Biblical account that God doesn't want your activity? *He wants your surrender.* Give it up to Him. Let Christ fight the battles for you. Be still and watch His activity. Trust that He knows the way through your wilderness journeys. And when you get pinned in a corner, watch Him intervene and see the new roads that are opened. He specializes in new highway construction!

PRAYER

Heavenly Father, I know that you bring crisis into my life for a purpose. Too often, I try to massage the fears that come without you. I haven't been still to see Your activity and the promises You want to give me over my enemies. Today, I'm choosing to stand still and watch You work. I want to see your testimony shine through my patience to the people in my world. Teach me the importance of letting You fight my battles for me. I want You to gain the glory in my life. If it means getting ahead of me to pull me along, do it. If it means getting behind me to push me forward, do that as well. I want to see you work things out in the days to come that will tell the world that You're still in charge. Thank you for being so patient with me! Help me to accept crisis as an opportunity to watch you shine in my life. May Christ get all the glory from this commitment that I make. In Your precious Son's Name, I pray. AMEN.

TALK TIME!

1. Name a crisis situation that produced a great amount of fear in your life. What do you remember about it? What were you inclined to do?
2. When you see in Exodus 14 how God engineered this crisis in

Israel's life, what does this mean to you? Apply this principle personally to your own daily situation.

3. Why is it so tense to leave our personal comfort zones?

4. Review the promises God offers during times of crisis. Which one do you need the most today? Be specific in your response.

5. There's an old proverb that says, "Lord give me patience, but please give it to me in a hurry?" Does this describe you? Why is it so hard to wait?

6. Comment on this sentence: "The simple truth is that you can't know God if you're too busy."

7. Do you know someone who is going through a time of crisis and fear in their life? How can this lesson equip you to help him/her?

9

TAKE THIS JOB AND LOVE IT

"So whether you eat or drink or whatever you do,
do it all for the glory of God."
1 Corinthians 10:31

There is an insightful story about an old farmer who owned a large plantation with two strong sons. One day, the aged homesteader knew that his life was coming to an end, so he called the two boys to his bedside. He said to them, "My sons, my farm and everything in it are yours in equal shares. I will leave you a little cash in the family bank, but the bulk of my inheritance is hidden somewhere in the ground, not more than eighteen inches from the surface. I regret that I've forgotten precisely where it lies."

After the father's funeral, the two sons began their work on the farm. With their broad forks and long shovels, they dug every inch of ground, looking for the buried treasure. They failed to find it, but in their search, they decided to sow a crop in the field as they dug deep. Everyday, they gave diligent effort to digging and sowing. This tough spadework produced loose, fertile soil. At the end of the growing season, they reaped a good crop, yet they found no hidden treasure. They decided to turn the soil deeply again in the search. Because of their work, the soil responded with another record crop, but no buried treasure surfaced. After three seasons turning the soil deeply, they soon discovered that their fields were producing the biggest cash crops in the county. Yet they found no sunken chest. So they continued their fortune hunt with diligent digging.

Year after year, they failed to find a real sunken treasure chest on their father's property. Yet their savings account increased significantly from season to season. Only in their later years did they learn what their father meant about buried wealth. Real treasure comes as a result of hard work.

A quick look over the landscape of our society will reveal how few people work hard these days. We've all seen people like this in one way or another. How often have you driven past work crews doing road or utility repair and seen one person doing the digging while three people are sitting around and watching him? We've all stood at the checkout line at the department store waiting for the cashier to serve us when an unimportant phone call keeps the cashier from ringing up our purchases. Not too long ago, I was standing at the men's department cashier *with money in my hand* to pay for a silk tie when the clerk's *boyfriend* called to talk. She didn't even acknowledge me! I waited for more than ten minutes! I felt like putting a flashing blue light on this station and voicing over the intercom, *"Attention customers! Come on over to the men's department and hear the 'Days of our Lives! For the next ten minutes, you'll get an additional ten percent discount!"* While you and I would like to do this at times, I'm sure the effort would be futile. This kind of attitude is prevalent everywhere. All of us can think of situations in the last few months where laziness, apathy and disinterest mark many job sites today.

Over the last twenty years, I've had the opportunity to talk and work with a wide range of people. Some were rich and prominent. Some made minimum wages flipping burgers and cooking fries. Others worked in large factories on shift schedules. I've interacted with people who work in office settings as well as with people who work outside in the elements to make a living. While some of these people were unemployed for a period of time, others had more work to do than they could handle. Yet one thing I heard repeatedly was *"I hate my job."* Some didn't like their boss. Others thought they should get more pay. I heard many say that they didn't like the type of work they were doing. Add to this situation a number of folks who disliked the people that worked around them. I remember some of these dissatisfied people vividly. Their faces and voices were etched with frustration, anger and disappointment over their daily duties.

I remember Paul's confession to our small group several years ago. He worked in a comfortable office setting with good people around him. Yet his clients were hard-to-satisfy people. In his mind, they were always out to get him. One day he broke down before us during our weekly breakfast Bible study and said, "Guys, I'm hurting at work. I hate what I do. I don't like the people I serve. I work long hours for average pay. I can't get time off. My family life has gone off the deep end. I'm in tense, spiritual pain. Where's God in all of this?"

That question echoes in my ears to this day. There are many who have voiced that same feeling. Perhaps you've felt it too. You're not alone. There are thousands who go to work each day feeling battered, pressured, pushed and beaten to submission. They wonder if life is even worth living, especially when nothing positive happens in their work environment. An older gentleman summed it up well to me, *"Son, if you're not happy with your work, you're not happy with your life."*

I want to look at this issue from a biblical point of view for three basic reasons. *The first reason deals with time percentage.* If roughly half or more of your waking hours are spent on the job, then you need to understand what God thinks about work. *The second reason deals with perspective.* Too many people view God as the Lord of their *church life* and not the Lord of their *work life.* Paul didn't have that distinction in mind when he wrote, *"So whether you eat or drink or whatever you do, do it all for the glory of God"* (I Corinthians 10:31). He meant for your daily work to glorify God just as much as your faithful participation in your local church. We need to stop this unbiblical dichotomy. Your work life should be viewed and understood from your understanding of God and His Word.

The third reason why we need to look at work deals with equipping. There are many who need help and hope on the job site. They need to gain some meaning to the work they do. Perhaps you're one of them. How can you become productive, satisfied and fulfilled from your job? Let's look at the Bible's perspective on work.

LESSON FOCUS

When we understand the biblical value of work against the common myths of our day, we'll discover that God established work to give us personal satisfaction and the resources needed to meet our needs and the needs of others. When we try to work as people created in the image of God, we'll come to know God, the Master Worker better and we'll receive greater motivation to labor harder and more diligently in our daily tasks. We'll give more effort to our job because we know that we'll give an account to the Lord someday for the things that were done with our hands and our minds.

CURRENT MYTHS ABOUT WORK[32]

American poet Benjamin Franklin King (1857-1894) aptly summarized many peoples' views about work when he wrote:

> Nothing to do but work,
> Nothing to eat but food,
> Nothing to wear but clothes
> To keep one from going nude.[33]

It seems that pessimism abounds in the work force today, especially among Christians who are trying to put Christ in the center of their daily responsibilities. Several myths that abound in the market place concerning the value of work rob them of enthusiasm in their job.

The first myth is that work is a part of the Genesis 3 curse. Somehow the idea has surfaced that work came because of the fall of Adam and Eve. Those that hold this view believe that since Adam disobeyed God's command, he was driven out of the Garden of Eden for the rest of his life to labor over insignificant duties because of his rebellion, believing that before Adam sinned, he lived with uninterrupted ease before God. Taken to its logical extreme, one can deduce from this view that if Adam had not sinned, he would never have worked. Those who hold to this position see work as a punishment in life; they believe we labor because we live under judgment.

While it is true that the fall of man brought a deadly curse upon the earth, it's not correct to say that work came *after* Adam's sin and

---

[32] A good book to read about a biblical theology of work is *Your Work Matters to God* by Doug Sherman and William Hendricks (NavPress, 1987). Some ideas are derived from this book.

[33] Benjamin Franklin King, "The Pessimist"

fall. A closer examination of Genesis 2 reveals that Adam received a job from his Creator-God *before* he sinned. In Genesis 2:15 we read, *"The Lord God took the man and put him in the Garden of Eden to work it and take care of it."* Long before sin entered the world through Adam's disobedience, God gave man a task to do. This ordinance of labor, along with marriage (2:24) and the Sabbath (2:2-3) formed the foundation for harmony, order and structure in society prior to the entrance of sin into the world. Work is not a part of the curse. It's part of God's original creation.

The curse of God in Genesis 3 focuses not on work itself, but *on the ground* (3:17). Because of the fall, thorns and thistles came to the harvest fields of the earth, driving people to work harder and longer (3:19). Although the *nature* of work was not changed with the fall, the *intensity* of work increased because of Adam's rebellion. Labor is not a curse. It's a part of the created order of God.

A second myth is that work is a temporal necessity. I've seen adult Sunday School teachers point to specific verses in the Old Testament to prove their point. As they read the following verses, they conclude that work is a necessary evil in society. Humans work not to gain achievement or to accomplish a goal, but to keep the bill collectors off their backs.

> *"Yet when I surveyed all that my hands had done and what I had toiled to achieve, everything was meaningless, a chasing after the wind; nothing was gained under the sun. What does a man get for all the toil and anxious striving with which he labors under the sun?"*
> (Ecclesiastes 2:11,22).

These words from King Solomon are often given to support the belief that even the wisest man that ever lived viewed work as an irrelevant exercise. It gives no purpose for living. You can give it your best shot, but when all is said and done, it's nothing but a worthless battle. There is no value or satisfaction in a day's labor.

While a surface reading of these and other passages in Ecclesiastes could persuade a person to formulate such a premature view, a closer study of the context of the book as a whole will not support this claim. Solomon's aim in this poetic treatise is to show *the futility of life and work without God at the center.* He attempts

to show in this book how God alone can give meaning and enjoyment in life (2:26). Satisfaction from work comes as a gift from
God's hand (3:13); Therefore, the only way to find fulfillment from
earthly existence and labor is to fear and to obey God (12:13). Work
has eternal value with the Lord as its foundation. You can only gain
fulfillment when your life is found in Him.

*A third myth is that the only work which is important is voca-
tional Christian work.* For years, an emerging view that continues
to gain an audience is that "church work" is superior to "secular
work." Sadly, this opinion has come from several known Christian
leaders who have considerable influence over the body of Christ.
Perhaps not realizing its potential danger, some Christian teachers
have suggested that vocational Christian work occupies a closer
place to the heart of God than the work done in the marketplace.
One of my favorite writers suggests this view:

> The work of preaching is the highest and the greatest and
> the most glorious calling to which anyone can ever be
> called.[34]

I'm trying not to take this quotation out of context but it brings
out an issue that wars within me. On the one hand, *I agree with
him completely*. The ministry of the gospel is certainly one of the
greatest privileges in the Kingdom of God. Part of me knows the
eternal value of Christian work as it relates to the extension of
God's kingdom on earth. At times I know that only God can call
and empower a person to do His work with faithfulness and fruitfulness. God's doesn't just pick "Normal Norms" and "Plain
Janes" to equip the saints for the work of the ministry. I'm convinced that He chooses Christian workers carefully. The Apostle
Paul even taught that a pastor should receive double honor
(1 Timothy 5:17). There is great value in being able to work in
the Christian ministry. Part of me understands and affirms this
principle.

At the same time, a Christian pastor or church staff member is
NOT on a different spiritual level from a believing coal miner in

---

[34] D. Martyn Lloyd-Jones, *Preaching and Preachers* (Zondervan, 1971), p. 9.

Kentucky or a garbage truck driver in New York City who professes Christ as Lord. If that coal miner or garbage truck driver senses God's calling to work his job and if a pastor feels the Lord's direction to preach in the pulpit, *both are fulfilling their role and function in life.* "Secular" work done for the glory of God *is distinctively Christian.* There is no fundamental difference in the value of work done in the church or in the marketplace if God is involved in the task.

The issue behind all of this is *calling.* What has God called you to do? Do you know in your heart what He has designed you to do? Have other believers commented on your strengths and interests? Do the people closest to you think that you're doing the right thing? If there are negative or uncertain thoughts in your spirit, you need to look into it. You may be doing secular business when God wants you to serve in a church or parachurch capacity. On the other hand, some may have entered a form of Christian ministry as an escape because they don't want to deal with specific issues in the marketplace. In either case, *you need to know your calling.* God calls some people to the formal Christian ministry just as He calls others to the business world. Both are important because they provide exposure to people who need to see God's light in us.

WHAT MAKES WORK SO VALUABLE?

God originally designed work to bring satisfaction and value to human life. By participating in the labor ordinance, we can learn important lessons about God, community and self-esteem. These lessons form the foundation for a proper theology of work.

The first lesson we can learn from work is the character of God. Have you ever thought of the first verse of the Bible as a great picture of work? In Genesis 1:1 we read, *"In the beginning, God created the heavens and the earth.* The first thing God ever wanted people to know about Him was His work. He "created!" From the beginning of time, God showed Himself not only as a Sovereign Lord and King over all things, but also as one who works out a plan to accomplish a goal. In Genesis, this plan involved the creation of living things. And as you survey the Bible, God is seen as an active workman, sustaining creation (Colossians 1:16-17), carrying out

His purpose in history (Ephesians 1:9-10), raising the Lord Jesus from the dead (Romans 10:9), accomplishing salvation through Christ's atonement (John 4:34) and bringing back the souls of believers with Jesus when He returns (1 Thessalonians 4:14). Because God is a worker, we learn more of God's character when we work like Him.

The fact that we are created in the image of God makes legitimate work an occupation of dignity. When we labor over an assigned task with faithfulness and discipline, we do something that is very Godlike.[35] We learn valuable lessons about our lives and about the character of God who made us to be workers. In other words, your work can help you know God better.

The second lesson we can learn from work is personal satisfaction. Within each of us, there rests a need not only for the presence of God but also for personal significance. God created humanity with a need for personal fulfillment. This significance and meaning comes as we walk with God and do the things He gives us to do. You see in Genesis 1:28-29 how God desires to give man fulfillment through his assigned work.

> *Then God said, "Let us make man in our image, according to our likeness; and let them rule over the fish of the sea and over the birds of the sky and over the cattle and over all the earth, and over every creeping thing that creeps on the earth." And God blessed them; and God said to them, "Be fruitful and multiply, and fill the earth, and subdue it; and rule over the fish of the sea and over the birds of the sky, and over every living thing that moves on the earth." Then God said, "Behold, I have given you every plant yielding seed that is on the surface of the earth, and every tree which has fruit yielding seed; it shall be food for you; and to every beast of the earth and to every bird of the sky and to everything that moves on the earth which has life, I have given every green plant for food;" and it was so.*

---

[35] *Your Work Matters to God*, p. 81.

Before leaving the first chapter of the Bible, you quickly learn that God wants to give people significance, fulfillment and enjoyment in life. This satisfaction is found through the work that God gives. Work was instituted by God to inject contentment and value in life.

You'll never be satisfied in life until you're doing the things you know in your heart that God has called you to do. If God chooses you to be a homemaker (one of the most valuable professions in life), the greatest fulfillment you'll ever receive in your life is when you run your home with faithfulness, consistency and love. If God calls you to the business world, do everything you can with the resources available to you. If you do, God will make your life count. If He sovereignly leads you to work on an assembly line, make a commitment to work hard each day as a witness for Christ and you'll leave satisfied. If you're happy with your work, most likely you'll be happy with your life.

A third lesson we can learn from work is the opportunity to help others. The Apostle Paul reminded his young disciple Timothy that a person who does not provide for his own family has denied the faith and lives worse than an unbeliever (1 Timothy 5:8). Through the legitimate labor that God gives us, we are to support those who are closest to us first. But it doesn't stop there. We need to help those around us in their times of need as well. Paul wrote in Ephesians 4:28, *"He who has been stealing must steal no longer, but must work, doing something useful with his own hands, that he may have something to share with those in need."* Through our work, we are to support our loved ones first and then share with others in need as God directs us and blesses our work.

Jesus said to his disciples, *"freely you have received, freely give"* (Matthew 10:8b). The context of this passage centers in the commission that He gave them before they were sent to do kingdom work. In their calling, they were told to "heal the sick, raise the dead, cleanse those who have leprosy and drive out demons" as they preached the gospel. In other words, when they went out to work (i.e. doing these things in conjunction with the preaching of the gospel), they would see amazing things happen. People would be touched; lives would be changed. Others would benefit from their actions. Yes, there would be hardships and sacrifice. Not everyone would welcome them, but they would make a great difference in the lives of many people. People would see God in their actions. Likewise in our own commissions, God calls us to our specific tasks in order that we may give freely to other people. People are one of the major reasons why God gives us work. We were never meant to live and to work in a vacuum. We were designed to labor so that our families, our loved ones and others could receive blessing and help to keep them going.

A fourth reason we can learn from work is the witness it gives to Christ. God created us to glorify Him not only in our living, but also in our work. Paul makes this point clear in 1 Corinthians 10:31, *"So whether you eat or drink or whatever you do, do it all for the glory of God."* Since roughly half of your daily waking hours are centered in your job, you need to see that one of the greatest ways God can receive honor is through the tasks you do before others. This forms a solid foundation for appropriate relational evangelism. People stand a greater chance of listening to the gospel when they see a job well done from you.

God wants His glory seen in the work we do. The reason is simple—His presence in the lives of His people in the work place serves as a great evangelistic vehicle for the extension of His kingdom. *One of the greatest mission fields in the world is the job site where you work.* Unchurched unbelievers face the greatest possibility of meeting Jesus Christ *as they watch your evangelistic work.* If you do your tasks with God's glory in mind, the odds are strong that eventually you'll get an opportunity to *speak evangelistic words.* The key is watching and waiting. Through our daily jobs, we can glorify God and extend His kingdom *by what we do and say.*

A WORK MODEL THAT HONORS GOD

Now that we see the biblical value of work, it's important to look at a role model for work that honors God in the marketplace. It may surprise you that Rebekah, the beautiful wife of Isaac, serves as a fantastic example for work that brings attention and glory to God. Her actions deserve careful examination and application to our own work environments. In Genesis 24, we discover the occasion that compels her to work diligently and faithfully.

We learn from this account that Abraham was very old. His wife, Sarah, was dead, buried in the cave of Machpelah. Concerned for his son Isaac, he commissions his chief servant to search for Isaac's wife back in his own country in Northwest Mesopotamia. Cultural conditions in that day required the parents to do the match -making work in marriage. To us it seems odd; however, the more I study this practice and watch my own three children grow up to adulthood, the more I see the validity of this procedure. Let the parents pick!

Abraham's head servant, realizing the immensity of his task, swore an oath to his master and journeyed back to his home country in search of Isaac's wife. When he arrived in the town of Nahor, he waited near the well outside the city so he could examine the women who came to draw water at the end of the day. While he was praying to God for guidance, a beautiful woman came to the well with an empty jar. Compelled to approach her, Abraham's servant asked for a drink of water. Without hesitation, Rebekah not only satisfied his personal thirst, but also watered his ten camels that were kneeling close to the well. From this experience, the servant discovered that this young woman was from Abraham's line, a perfect match for Isaac; and the turnkey for this discovery came when she went out of her way to show hospitality to him and to his delegation.

I've reviewed enough commentaries on this passage to conclude that a major part of the narrative goes unnoticed. What gets left out? Rebekah's work ethic! Too many times, Bible teachers look at this story and focus *only* on the theme of the providential working of God in securing a wife for Isaac. Certainly that's understood from the bird's eye scheme of things, but in the *immediate context*, Abraham's servant is the recipient of some hard work! Rebekah not only satisfied his own thirst, but *also* the thirst of his ten camels. Think of the needs of not one, but *ten camels*. A camel can store an enormous amount of water, yet Rebekah had only one jar to fill and to pour. There's no telling *how many times* she drew water from that city well to satisfy the servant's caravan. Also factor to this equation the *long journey* that Abraham's delegation took to arrive in the City of Nahor. One estimate puts it over 500 miles[36]—*on camels!* These

---

[36] Henry Morris, *The Genesis Record* (Baker, 1976), p. 393

animals were thirsty!

There's no telling how long Rebekah worked in this account; however, one thing is sure. *She went the second mile in helping a stranger she didn't know; yet she never complained.* There's much in her example that needs spotlighting. If a Christian's work ethic followed her pattern, *more businesses would come looking for believers to work for them.* Employers would hire followers of Jesus Christ *first* because their reputation would circulate as people who worked harder, longer and faster. One of the most powerful ways a Christian can witness for the Lord is through consistent, diligent, faithful work. This work ethic builds a platform upon which credible words of the gospel can be shared with others. Hard work done with a good attitude draws people's attention. It builds trustworthiness, giving any believer an opportunity to tell others about Christ in a credible setting. But keep this in mind. *A consistent, diligent work ethic is a prelude to sharing the gospel.* Don't fall for the trap that says, "I witness by my life, not my words." It's not one or the other. *It's both.* On the one hand, speaking the gospel without a good work ethic will not gain a credible hearing. On the other hand, the world perceives a good work ethic without a deliberate gospel witness as only *good morality*, and good morality has nice intentions. The problem is they send people to hell!

We need more role models like Rebekah in the work place. There must be this diligent, do-whatever-it-takes-attitude in the minds of God's people to make a difference in the world. All too often, I'm afraid Christians have allowed themselves to camouflage with others in the job market so that the world can't see the difference. You don't see this with Rebekah. You don't see it in the Apostle Paul. Most importantly, you don't see it in the life of Jesus. He said to the disciples in His Sermon on the Mount, *"If someone forces you to go one mile, go with him two miles"* (Matthew 5:41). Do your job with diligence. Labor with intensity. *Work hard AND smart.* You never know who's watching.

THE CHRISTIAN WORK ETHIC—A THEOLOGY FOR SMART, HARD WORK

There is an old Chinese proverb that says, "A man grows most tired while standing still." God never created us to live idle lives. He made us so that through our relationship to Him and through our work, we would find meaning in life. The writer of Proverbs warned that lazy hands produce poverty while diligent hands bring prosperity (Proverbs 10:4). Paul wrote that if a man didn't work, he shouldn't eat (2 Thessalonians 3:10). How does this apply to Christians in the marketplace? Why work hard? What should drive a Christian to give quality work?

The first reason revolves around a believer's personal accountability to Christ in light of His Second Coming. Throughout the New Testament, believers were continually reminded that the Lord's return meant accountability to Him before His judgment seat. Paul wrote in 2 Corinthians 5:10, "For we must all appear before the judgment seat of Christ, that each one may receive what is due him for the things done while in the body, whether good or bad." Notice the thrust of this accountability is on things accomplished in life. He doesn't say "things thought" or "things imagined." He says "things DONE." He continues this theme in 1 Corinthians 3:12-15, "If any man builds on this foundation using gold, silver, costly stones, wood, hay or straw, his work will be shown for what it is, because the Day will bring it to light. It will be revealed with fire, and the fire will test the quality of each man's work. If what he has built survives, he will receive his reward. If it is burned up, he will suffer loss; he himself will be saved, but only as one escaping through the flames." The fact that I will have to give an account to my Master for the labors of my hands and heart should be a driving force behind my work ethic. I should want to work smart and hard because I know that Christ will reward His servants for their faithfulness and fruitfulness in God's world. From a biblical perspective, there is a relationship between smart work AND hard work. Because I know I will give an account to Christ at His judgment seat, I work with focus, planning and effort. This means through prayer, I envision God's goals for the work He has for me to do, apply His wisdom in formulating priorities for this labor and give my heart fully to this endeavor while the other areas of my life (marriage, family, church, personal rest) are kept in balance. Biblical work is inspected work. You see this in several of Jesus' parables (Matthew 21:34, 25:19, Luke 19:15). End times accountability should motivate me to work hard and smart because I want to receive a reward in order to give it back to Him in worship. I don't want to be left empty-handed before His presence. I want to give Him something!

There's also another way to look at this truth. According to the 1 Corinthians 3 passage, poor work will not survive as it's passed through the eternal accountability flames. In fact it says those that follow this track *will suffer loss*. It's hard to have a full understanding of this picture, but I do know that I don't want to appear before the One who gave me His all and to show Him *that I didn't give Him my all*. I don't want to barely make it! I've got time *now* to make a difference! Smart, hard work done for the glory of God is a personal investment in eternity!

While this first reason is somewhat futuristic in thinking, there's another reason that strikes closer to home in a more immediate way. It has to do with *the deep impact of the gospel upon my daily personal life*. Jesus Christ loved me in the greatest way by coming to this earth as the world's greatest worker. He worked out God's plan of salvation by living to the peak of his adult years and then by *dying for me*. No greater love could ever be given than for someone to die for another person. Yet that's what Jesus did for me! He sacrificed and worked for me! If I were the only person who ever lived, Jesus would still have come! Therefore *no personal sacrifice or work for Him is too great*. My life has been deeply impacted by the gospel of His work and it will never be the same. Because He did all this for me, I want to make a difference *TODAY*—in the lives of those around me. And one of the best ways I can do this is by the work that He has called me to do. Diligent, faithful work shows that I'm working and living *with a purpose*. God has touched me and I want to impact others with His life-changing power in what I do and say.

Can you say that today? Has Jesus made a personal difference in your life? Does your work reflect the diligence of His work for you? Do you want to receive a reward before His judgment seat so that you can offer Him a gift in worship? It's time to think of the importance of your job. God doesn't have you there by mistake. He wants you to work hard and to work smart everyday on the job while keeping the other areas of your life (marriage, family, other relationships and responsibilities) in balance. This isn't a prescription for workaholism; rather it's an attempt to look at work from a biblical point of view and to see how we can receive proper motivation to do the kind of work that pleases the Lord. Biblical work is faithful, fruitful productive work done with balance. God really wants you to take your job and to love it the way He loves you! So roll up your sleeves, make out a plan and charge ahead! Make this workday your most productive ever! You're investing in your eternity!

SUMMARY

We have surveyed several current myths about work. While many believe that labor is meaningless and part of the curse upon man, God presents work as valuable and significant in His sight. Through work, we come to know Christ better and to see how we can support our families and those in need around us. By looking at Rebekah's work ethic, we learn the importance of going the extra mile and doing the additional things that bring glory to God. There is a strong biblical work ethic that should compel us to give diligence to all our daily responsibilities. Jesus is coming back. I will have to give an account to Him of my labors. More specifically, He has impacted my life and I want to make a difference for Him *today*. Nothing is too great for me to do for Him.

APPLICATION

Jesus' words make an important point that we need to apply. He said, *"Well **done**, good and faithful servant!"* (Matthew 25:21a, my emphasis). He didn't say, "Well *said*" or "Well *thought*." *He said, "Well done."* He commended His servants for the fruitful, faithful work that was entrusted to their care. Can that be said of you? Are your motives for work biblical? Do people around you think you're productive or lazy? Do you work in the light of the Second Coming? Are you working today with the realization that you will stand before Jesus at the judgment seat of believers? Can others see the impact of Jesus in your work and in your attitude toward your work? Spend some time evaluating your life and your work and make a commitment to give Christ your best effort today. He did His best work for you!

PRAYER

Heavenly Father, you've given me a lot to think about when it comes to my work. Forgive me for accepting some of the modern day myths about work. Today, I want to model the importance of faithful, fruitful work that pleases you. Show me the areas where I need to be more diligent. Produce in me a godly attitude that will go the second mile as Jesus did for me. Help me to work as if Christ my Master would come back today for an accounting. I want to show others the deep impact of the gospel in my personal life by the way I handle my daily job. Fill me with your Holy Spirit and enable me to work hard and to work smart, looking for opportunities to share the gospel building on the credibility of my labors. While I work, help me to keep the other areas of my life in balance and to remember the place they occupy in my life. I want to give you the glory for the labors of my hands and my heart. Thank you for giving me something to do in this life until you return. I dedicate my job and my daily attitude toward it into Your hands. In Your name I pray. AMEN.

TALK TIME!

1. What myths have you heard about work out in the marketplace or business world? What do most people you know think about work?
2. Comment on this sentence: "Too many people view God as the Lord of their *church life*, but not the Lord of their *work life*."
3. Review the section on the Biblical value of work. Which one(s) strike home to you?
4. Is it really possible to know God deeper through the work that we do?
5. What strikes you about Rebekah's example in Genesis 24? Comment on this thought: "If a Christian's work ethic followed her pattern, *more businesses would come looking for believers to work for them.* Employers would hire followers of Jesus Christ *first* because their reputation would circulate as people that worked harder, longer and faster." Do you agree or disagree? Why?

6. Evaluate the section on the Christian work ethic. Why should a believer work hard? Is this really important?
7. Do you know people who are struggling with their jobs? How can this lesson equip you to help them?

PART 2:

GOD'S HELP FOR MY FAMILY LIFE

10

BUT WE DON'T LOVE ONE ANOTHER ANYMORE

"Finally, all of you, live in harmony with one another; be sympathetic, love as brothers, be compassionate and humble."
1 Peter 3:8

Not too long ago, I was watching a nature television show that documented the history of a four hundred-year-old tree in Colorado. Commentators remarked that when Columbus discovered the New World, this tree was merely a sapling against the rugged Colorado landscape. For four centuries, this majestic giant endured fourteen lightening strikes, numerous wind storms and even a moderate earthquake. It won over all the outward elements and forces; however, it's life came to an end because of an inward enemy.

Scientists detected that the tree was dying and would soon fall to the ground. So they positioned cameras at several key lookout spots to film the mighty plunge. Not too long after the setup, the giant hardwood tumbled over in a spectacular drop. Immediately after the fall, the research team came close to the base of the great tree. As they approached the base, they noticed thousands of tiny black beetles scurrying from hole to hole, chewing and burrowing their teeth into the tree's rich fibers. Scientists couldn't tell how long they lived there. They simply concluded that one beetle found a soft spot in the tree's armor and summoned all his friends to join him for a full course meal three times a day. From their persistent diet, this towering giant's life came to a perilous end.

The thing that struck me about this show was *the way the tree died*. It wasn't a major "crisis" event (lightening strikes, earthquake, etc.) that ended its existence. Instead, it was the little, daily things (the beetles) that chewed decay into its life. Before you knew it, those daily things produced serious health problems that drained life from the tree's base. No one could see that there were major problems until it was too late. Everything looked good for a long time. But inside, life was attacked and devoured.

I see this principle often in the marriages of people I know such as Ron and Jeanette. Ron was a successful account executive with a large CPA firm. Jeanette was a receptionist for a hair and nail salon. During several months of the season, Ron worked virtually around the clock in his office just to keep his nose above water. One night, he checked his e-mail and found an invitation to explore a pornographic web-site. Feeling a sense of relief over finishing a major case and thinking it wouldn't harm him, he clicked the button and saw things he never saw before in his life. Before he knew it, he was traveling daily to many web-sites in an attempt to satisfy his new-found addiction. He didn't think that this tiny problem would last long. "I'll get my fill of this and then move on to something else," he said. He didn't know at the time that his infatuation with this practice produced withdrawal feelings from Jeanette, leaving her feeling alone.

While Ron engaged in this secret practice late at night, Jeanette met the newest fitness trainer at the health club in the adjacent building. One day while he was waiting for his haircut appointment, he and Jeanette started a conversation that became intensely personal in a matter of minutes. She had never had someone so genuine talk to her like this guy did. Because Ron was busy doing CPA work all the time, they didn't have time for one another. They were living under the same roof, but they were drifting away from one another. The kids knew something was wrong, but couldn't figure out why mom and dad were out all the time.

It wasn't long before each other's activities were revealed. Feeling guilty for not being at home for four straight nights, Ron stopped by the hair salon on Friday to take Jeanette out to lunch. She wasn't there, but someone told him that she went to the restaurant down the street with this new fitness trainer. When he came to the diner, he could see both of them conversing at a private booth.

He could see that they were enjoying one another and that their eyes were glued to each other. He approached the table and confronted Jeanette and demanded an explanation. "Why are you here with this person?" he asked. With a sinister look in her eyes, she squinted back at him and said, "The same reason why you watch what you do on the Internet." Before you knew it, both sides were shouting at one another and walking out of the restaurant.

Word spread quickly around town about the incident. I learned about it less than eight hours after it happened. Since Ron was a deacon in the church, I called and asked to see him and Jeanette immediately. They agreed to let me come over and talk with them. Several minutes went by before both of them looked at me and essentially said, "We just don't love one another anymore." My heart sank as I looked at two people who had virtually everything that anyone could ever want, yet were empty on the inside, headed for disaster.

What would you have told Ron and Jeanette? I heard some of the street talk opinions about them. There were some who said, "Well, if you don't love one another, then it's time to depart. He needs to go his way, and she needs to go her way." Some blamed it on Ron. Others wanted to throw stones on Jeanette. A third group pointed the judgment finger on the fitness trainer while a final group shown the spotlight on the computer. "It's the Internet's fault," they say. "It's too strong a temptation."

As I sat in their beautiful living room, I could feel the anger in the air. You could cut the tension with a knife while you heard the applause of hell. Like the science team approaching the fallen tree, I was seeing the inner organisms that had eaten the insides of their marriage. Their relationship, like that tree, was dead. I asked myself, "What can I do now? Their lives have fallen. 'Timber!' had been declared. I knew their kids were running for cover. What could I possibly do right now?"

At that moment, something hit me. It's as if someone said to me, "If you will tell them the sin of their lives and show them what I say about marriage, I can do a work in their lives." I looked at both of them and told them lovingly but forcefully, "You are both in sin. Until you recognize in both of your lives that you have not betrayed one another, but also God, you will never experience restoration in your lives. *God is calling you to repent now.*"

Something special happened that moment. A spirit of brokenness blew into that room. Ron burst into tears. Jeanette fell to the floor and began to sob uncontrollably. I led them in prayer and sensed that something genuine was happening. After thirty minutes of prayer and confession (something this couple never did), we arose from the living room and went to the dining room table. God was on the hunt and reclaimed another marriage from the grave. A new shoot came out of that old dead tree. Once I sensed that their confession and repentance was genuine, I was led to share 1 Peter 3 with them.

The first seven verses of 1 Peter 3 give one of the fuller presentations of the proper role between husband and wife in the marriage relationship. This passage greatly helped Ron and Jeanette to reclaim their relationship under the banner of Christ. I know it can help you or another couple you know who are struggling in a relationship and asking the question, "God, where are you when we don't love one another anymore?"

LESSON FOCUS

From 1 Peter 3, we can discover the ways husbands and wives can woo each other back into a healthy marriage relationship. As wives focus on their character and behavior and base it in the hope of God's intervention, they can receive assurance that God is pleased with their motives and that their husbands will come back to them. As husbands focus on understanding and respecting the physical, emotional, spiritual and in some cases the professional dimensions of their wives and give tangible expressions of appreciation, thoughtfulness and empathy to them as a matter of daily living, they can know that God is pleased with their intentions and will reward them with answered prayer. The key to success lies in the deliberate intentional actions of both parties.

HOW WIVES CAN WIN THEIR HUSBANDS

Notice in the middle of 1 Peter 3:1 that the apostle tells the married women in his audience that there are ways to "win over" their husbands. While the traditional interpretation of this passage views the idea of "winning over" as the claiming of their soul for Christ, I also believe another dimension of understanding is possible. I think this passage teaches a woman how to influence her husband to come to Christ *and how to influence him to come back to her heart in the marriage relationship.* After all, if she is a believer and he is an unbeliever, how much tension is there already? Much! The principles Peter tells them to do in the first six verses can ignite a spiritual and emotional change in the husband to return to the Lord and his wife with love and devotion.

The first way to win a husband back is through behavior. The text tells us in verse 1, *"Wives, in the same way be submissive to your husbands so that, if any of them do not believe the word, they may be won over without talk by the **behavior** of their wives."* Ladies, listen to this because it's crucial for understanding how you can make inroads back into your man's life. *The way you win over your husband's heart is not with your tongue. It's with your temperament.* Your behavior is seen in the *outward* actions of your life. One way you win the love and admiration of your husband is through the simple things you do that make him know that he's the greatest. By "simple," *I don't mean simplistic.* These behavioral principles are quite profound! When I say "simple," I mean something that is *clear and understandable.* If you will practice these with heart and devotion, the man in your house will take notice.

BEHAVIORAL PRINCIPLES THAT PAY DIVIDENDS

A key behavior that pays dividends in the marriage relationship is *submission.* Peter mentions it twice in the text (v.1, 5). What is submission? From everything we hear in the world, it's not attractive or desirable. It conjures up thoughts of women being used and abused like a doormat. Many have twisted the meaning of this word to force women to do all kinds of things, all in the effort to make them bow to their husbands.

What is the central thought truly embedded in submission? *In reality, it's something men don't want to admit because it deals with spiritual leadership in the home, something most of them don't do very well.* Paul wrote in Ephesians 5:22, *"Wives, submit to your* *husbands **as to the Lord***" (my emphasis). Submission at its very core simply means that a woman acknowledges her husband as the spiritual head of the home and that he is responsible to lead her and the family in the direction God sets for them. *And she is letting him do it.* Ladies, before God, you and your husband stand as equals when it comes to relationships. But when it comes to *roles*, the husband is the head. Submission means acknowledging that he's in charge of the spiritual direction of the home and letting him lead.

This issue continues to draw tremendous heat from unbelievers *and believers* in our world today. In November 1999, the Texas Baptist Convention rejected submission as a necessary part of a woman's role in marriage. In the minds of many of the convention's pastors and leaders, submission is an irrelevant practice in our western culture. They believe it's confined only as a first century Middle Eastern custom. Women should not fall prey to this admonition because of it's potential harm to their personal life.

So much of the misunderstanding surrounding this principle centers around the misuse of this meaning and the lack of seeing the *dual responsibilities involved in the marriage relationship.* While a woman is supposed to be "submitting" (acknowledging her husband's spiritual lead), her husband in turn is to be loving and cherishing her at the same time. Check me out on this, but I don't think you'll find teaching about a woman submitting to her husband *all by itself in a passage.* Any reference to women's submission always includes specific reference to the affectionate care that a man should give to his wife. You see it here in 1 Peter 3 and also in Ephesians 5. The idea conveyed is that of *mutual devotion.* The man cares for his wife by loving her. The woman responds by following her man's lead. When both of these are going on, you see incredible love and peace in the home.

Is this the norm today? Obviously not, but it's the Scriptural pattern. This teaching is just as important today as it was in the First Century, yet just as tense. The real problems surface when one side doesn't fulfill their end of their marriage vows. Many times the man doesn't spiritually lead and show concern for the emotional and spiritual well being of his wife. Other times the wife is so driven to take charge that she doesn't accept the thoughtfulness from her husband. It's imperative to note the *order of the teaching.* In both Paul and Peter, *the woman's role is mentioned first.* These apostles envisioned that there would be times when the man would not spiritually care and lead his family in the direction of the Lord. In these and other situations, the principle remains firm. Ladies, acknowledge your husband's spiritual lead and let him do it. Don't step in for him, let him lead. If he doesn't want to lead or is leading you in the wrong direction, don't overrule him. Instead, *cry out to God on his behalf.* Get others to join you in this prayer. Petition the Lord Most High to come to your aid. Countless numbers of women will testify at this point that God does something when you give the problem to Him. He moves things around and makes things work together for good. By recognizing His control in your life in these situations, He is honored with your obedience and will give you the most incredible grace to deal with the issues of your husband's leadership (or lack thereof). I know it's not easy to accept this on a daily basis, but it's the truth. It's something that will cause you to deepen your walk with God if you will let Him.

Another key behavior that pays dividends is *purity of life.* In verse 2, Peter teaches wives to submit so that their husbands will be won over *"when they see the purity and reverence of your lives."* This doesn't simply refer to sexual purity from the world and loyalty to her spouse, but also to moral purity that starts with a genuine reverence for God. It's the same type of purity mentioned by Paul when he tells Timothy, *"Keep yourself pure"* (1 Timothy 5:22). Through genuine holiness and moral sanctity, a wife can win over her husband because character speaks in any generation. An upright life builds a platform of respect and credibility for the message you embody.

Horatius Bonar (1808-1889), the famous Scottish pastor, theologian and hymn writer, explains that this godliness is seen as a consecration to God in all walks of life:

> This holiness or consecration extends to every part of our persons, fills up our being, spreads over our life, influences everything we are, or do, or think, or speak, or plan, small or great, outward or inward, negative or positive, our loving, our hating, our sorrowing, our rejoicing, our recreations, our business, our friendships, our relationships, our silence, our speech, our reading, our writing,

our going out and our coming in—our whole man in every movement of spirit, soul, and body. In the house, the sanctuary, the chamber, the market, the shop, the desk, the highway, it must be seen that ours is a consecrated life.[37]

Through this kind of consecration and purity of life to Christ and to His truths, a wife can win over her husband through her behavior.

The second way to win a husband back is through character. In 1 Peter 3:3, the apostle tells the women not to draw beauty from outward fashion and cosmetic appeal which clearly reflect the primary path of today's world. Rather, he draws attention to an important truth in verse 4, *"Instead, it should be that of your inner self, the unfading beauty of a gentle and quiet spirit, which is of great worth in God's sight."* The inner self that Peter talks about is *character*. The inward actions of your life speak of the character of your spirit. You win the love and admiration of your husband when your private life is well ordered.

HOW CAN YOU KNOW IF YOUR PRIVATE LIFE IS IN ORDER?

The apostle appears to give two noticeable characteristics that can help a woman gauge whether her character is ordered and under the peaceful control of Christ in daily life. *The first sign is a gentle and quiet spirit.* Peter says such a spirit possesses great worth in God's sight. What is a gentle and quiet spirit? To state it simply, it means that a woman has a calm and unwavering assurance in God's grace. She doesn't strike back in vengeance, but rather puts her faith and security in the Lord to work out all things according to His plan and purpose (Romans 8:28). She accepts her lot in life and draws upon Christ's peace for meaning and value in her daily responsibilities. This dependence on Christ forms a channel that the Holy Spirit uses to transform her life as well as the lives of those around her. A woman who possesses this gentleness and quietness will have an ordered private life.

---

[37] Horatius Bonar, *God's Way of Holiness* (Evangelical Press, 1979), p. 10. This was first published in 1864. Write Evangelical Press, P.O. Box 5, Welwyn, Hertfordshire AL6 9NU, England.

What is the heart of gentleness and quietness? *It is a surrendered trust to the plan of God.* It's the kind of trust that accepts and follows God's way through the wilderness even though you can't see your way out. Let's face it—there are a number of good, godly women who have to put up with a number of grumpy, disgusting men! At times these men lead their families down the wrong road without realizing the significant dangers of their decisions. A woman of quietness and gentleness trusts God to shield her family and to keep them secure when faulty leadership could derail their future.

Another noticeable fruit of an ordered private life is a confident hope in God. Sarah and other holy women of the past are noted as positive examples of obedience and character before their watching husbands. By looking to Christ for assurance and strength, they received in return a confidence that gave security to the lives of those who lived in their home. Their husbands would see their submission and reliance upon God, and it would fuel them with passion and confidence to lead the home in a godly, moral way. A confident hope in God produces an opportunity for God to invade the home with meaning, purpose and value. This is a valuable indicator of an ordered private life in a woman's heart.

John Calvin, the famous pastor/theologian of the Protestant Reformation in France and Switzerland, wrote these encouraging words to show the relationship between faith and the troubles in life that most of us face at one time or another. These words can encourage many women to find their hope in God even when the road is rough.

> Faith does not certainly promise itself either length of years or honor or riches in this life, since the Lord willed that none of these things be appointed for us. But it is content with this certainty: that, however many things fail us that have to do with the maintenance of this life, God will never fail. Rather, the chief assurance of faith rests in the expectation of the life to come, which has been placed beyond doubt through the Word of God. Yet whatever earthly miseries and calamities await those whom God has embraced in his love, these cannot hinder his benevo-

lence from being their full happiness.[38]

The basis for this kind of hope is *a deep-seated security in God.* Ladies, the way you win your husbands to your sides starts with *your personal relationship to God.* When you understand His available grace and the relationship you have to Him because of your position in Christ, it will produce character qualities and an inner hope that will weather the storms that life brings. When you give deliberate effort to improve your walk with God, it will show in your attitude to and your relationship with your husband. The way you win him back doesn't start with your initiative to him. It begins with accepting God's initiative toward you.

HOW HUSBANDS CAN WIN THEIR WIVES

I am reminded of a time when I led a Sunday School assembly of Junior High students when the question was asked, "What does God say about marriage?" Instantly, an eighth grade boy uttered these words that revealed the times in his home: "Father, forgive them, for they know not what they do!" In some ways, I think this amusing answer describes the understanding many men have about their relationship to their wife—*they don't know what they're doing.* I confess I fall into that category at times. What biblical instructions does Peter give to husbands that can help them win the hearts of their wives?

The first way a husband can win his wife is through understanding. In 1 Peter 3:7, the command to *"be considerate"* comes from the Greek work "gnósis" which deals with the knowledge and understanding of truth in its application to daily life. In other words, husbands are to win their wives over by recognizing the elements that constitute their wife's world and by accepting them with consideration, sympathy and understanding. It means coming to terms with the many things that are a part of a woman's life—her physical life, her emotional life, her spiritual life and in many cases her professional life—then showing appreciation, thoughtfulness and empathy for the way they affect her daily life. This decision to understand a wife is *an act of the mind.* It is an intentional decision to examine and

---

[38] John Calvin, *Institutes of the Christian Religion* (Westminster Press, 1960), Vol. 1, Book 3, p. 574.

to comprehend the things that go on in a woman's world.

To those men who are married, when was the last time you examined your wife's world? What's in it? Do you know what's going on in her daily life? More importantly, *do you ask your wife about the things going on in her busy world?* Take a moment to think about the events and people that comprise her life at this point. What does she need? Is she shepherding small children in diapers? Is she the family taxi-driver for children in school? Is she lonely because all the children have grown and left for college? If she has a job, what kind of people does she work with daily? Are they pleasant or a pain in the neck? What factors would make her have a good day or a bad day when you come home for dinner? How is she doing physically? Is she exercising and sleeping well? Do the children put excessive pressure on her? Are there things you can spot that reveal signs of wear or tension in her life? In the Apostle Peter's mind, the key to showing consideration to your wife is to understand her world. This takes intentional effort to observe, to ask and to think of her needs before your own interests.

The second way a husband can win his wife is through respect. In the middle of verse 7, Peter tells them to *"treat them with respect."* While showing consideration deals with an act of the mind, *showing respect reveals an act of the heart.* It demonstrates an attitude that you value another person highly and that you want them to experience the best of the relationship. When you honor another person with dignity and esteem, you lift them to a higher level of worth and significance. Those are the checks and balances of a marriage relationship. Men, if you love your wife by honoring her, cherishing her, esteeming her, lifting her up, respecting her and valuing her above everyone else, *she'll follow you everywhere you go in true biblical submission.* But if you don't respect her, don't be surprised if she comes dragging behind with an embittered spirit. The key to a woman's submission to you is *to honor and respect her first.* If you lay down your life for her, she'll return the act to you.

Peter gives three specific reasons why a man needs to respect his wife in the marriage relationship. *The first reason is that she is the "weaker" partner.* By "weaker," the text doesn't necessarily mean inferior in terms of size or strength. A quick look around this world will show that there are some mighty tall, strong and muscular

women. Some are professional athletes, body builders and participate in TV "rastlin'" matches. So "weaker" can't mean frail or pow-
erless, but rather *vulnerable and delicate.* Like a fine piece of china,
a woman is a lovely treasure of art and beauty. But if you abuse her,
she is vulnerable to fracture and brokenness.

*The second reason why a man needs to respect his wife is because
of her value in God's sight.* Peter says in verse 7 that women are
"heirs with you of the grace of life." By disrespecting them, you are
hurting yourself. Why? Because they're a treasure of God's amazing grace. Men, God has some incredible things in store for you
through your wife! Some of the greatest treasures and riches of your
life will come from God to you *through the channel of your wife.* As
the Proverbs 31 writer stated, a wife of noble character is *"worth far
more than rubies."* Respect and love her and you'll get great value
in return.

*The third reason why a man needs to respect his wife is because
of the negative consequences that come when you don't do this.* At
the end of verse 7, the stark reality is sobering. Peter tells husbands
to treat their wives properly *"so that nothing will hinder your
prayers."* Men, if we don't respect our wives and treat them as valuable in God's sight, *God won't hear our prayers.* Keep in mind that
God *WILL* hear their prayers, but not ours. It's as if the Lord is saying to us, *"Men, if you know what's good for you, you better take
notice of this truth and heed its warning. If you don't take care of
your wife, I won't listen to you. You'll be left alone until you come
to your senses and take care of the most valuable thing that I ever
gave you. That woman in your house is very important to me."*

When you honor and respect your wife by invading her world
with sympathy in order to understand the things that make up her
life, you can win her to your side. When she is close to your heart,
God will not be far away. If you commit to this initiative, you'll
have a happy, fulfilling marriage that will stand against the trials of
life and you'll live with the greatest fulfillment that a human being
can experience in this life. When both parties of a marriage do their
part, it produces a relationship that has the breath of heaven in it.
Don't you want that today?

SUMMARY

We've seen from 1 Peter 3 how a married couple can win each other back to a healthy, satisfying relationship. In order for a woman to win back her husband, she must possess a gentle and quiet spirit through a submissive, caring and loving behavior. Her hope will be grounded in the knowledge of God's security and power. She won't attempt to influence her husband with foolish talk or improper persuasion, but rather her influence will come from a godly temperament that is rooted in the character of God. In her daily life, she works on her inward beauty so that her husband will see the fruit of her character. Her life is marked by trust in the security of God's protection.

In the same passage, we've also seen that the way a man wins the honor and respect of his wife is through his understanding and sympathy of the things that go on in her world. He is considerate of her needs and puts her cares above his own because he wants to live with divine favor. He knows that his wife is a valuable treasure from God and a channel of His incredible grace. If he doesn't treat her properly, God will not hear his prayers; therefore, he recognizes her vulnerability and exquisite value by esteeming her with significant honor and love before all people. When he loves her first and takes care of her needs, she will follow him in true submission wherever he goes.

APPLICATION

What kinds of attitudes are seen in your marriage? Is there a mutual respect and love for one another? Men, do you *really* show love and value to your wives? Do you treat them as a delicate, valuable treasure in the sight of God? Do you sense that God is answering your prayers? If not, you may need to start with your marriage relationship! Take some time to know *HER* world. Find out about the people and the things that make up her day. Realize that some of the greatest blessings that will come to your life and family will come from God *through her*. She is your key to a happy, fulfilling life. Don't forget it! Treat her like a queen!

Women, work on your inward beauty. Cultivate a reverence for God and a pure, moral character. Let your husbands see your submissive behavior to them as an act of your devotion to God. Follow the example of great women in the past and support your husband's spiritual leadership. Even if he is not leading or if he is leading you in the wrong direction, *trust God anyway.* Put your hope in His caring hands and He will not let you down. He honors those who submit to His divine plan for the family. When you walk in God's path with God's wisdom, you will receive God's blessing on your home.

PRAYER

Heavenly Father, I want your blessing on my marriage. Help me to be the person You created me to be. Develop my inner life so that it is well ordered and pleasing to you. Give me the desire to know more about my spouse's world. Help me to find out about the people and the things that make up his/her life while I'm away from him/her. Give me the compassion of Christ to treat my spouse as a valuable treasure in your sight. I want to receive your blessing on my home. Grant that the Spirit and peace of Christ will overshadow our home and that people will be drawn to you because our marriage is rooted and grounded in the joy of Christ. Bless my spouse today in everything he/she does so that glory will come to Your great name. I ask this in the precious name of my Savior. AMEN.

TALK TIME!

1. How many people like Ron and Jeanette do you know today? What are the common reasons that cause marriages to deteriorate and to break up today in your community?
2. What are the everyday ideas that people give about "submission?" When you see the importance of *mutual devotion* (the husband loves and cares while the wife responds by following her husband's leadership), how does this motivate each party to do their best in the relationship?
3. Women, how hard is it to trust God when you see your husband's leadership taking you and the family in the wrong direction? What do you do in this situation?
4. Men, how can you get to know your wife's world more? Be

specific.

5. Women, what are some ways that you can encourage your husband in his spiritual leadership role? Be specific and realistic. How can you say this to him in an effective and supporting way?

6. Men, what are the qualities that make your wife so valuable? Be specific and encouraging. How can you communicate this to her in a kind and affectionate way?

7. Do you know a couple who is struggling in their marriage relationship? How can this lesson equip you to help them?

11

TRAIN A CHILD IN
THE WAY OF HIS GOING

*"Train a child in the way he should go, and when he is old
he will not turn from it."*
Proverbs 22:6

One of my favorite newspaper comics is the "Blondie" cartoon. In one episode, Dagwood says to Elmo, "How's your new baby sister?" Elmo replies, "She hasn't stopped crying since she came home from the hospital." In the next frame, a puzzled Dagwood says, "Why do you suppose she cries so much?" With frustration written all over his face, Elmo says, "If you had no hair, no teeth and were wet all the time, you'd cry too."

How many crying nights do you remember? Bill Cosby, the famous comedian, summed it up well when he wrote, "There is no commitment in the world like having children. Even though they often will drive you to consider commitment of another kind, the value of a family still cannot be measured."[39] What makes children so demanding at times? Consider the following story and see if it doesn't ring a bell inside you.

WHY PARENTS HAVE GREY HAIR

The boss of a big company needed to call one of his employees about an urgent problem with one of the main computers. He dialed

---

[39] Bill Cosby, *Fatherhood.* (Berkley Books), p. 158.

the employee's home phone number and was greeted with a child's whispered, "Hello?" Feeling put out at the inconvenience of having to talk to a youngster, the boss asked, "Is your Daddy home?" "Yes", whispered the small voice.

"May I talk with him?" the man asked.

To the surprise of the boss, the small voice whispered, "No."

Wanting to talk with an adult, the boss asked, "Is your Mommy there?"

"Yes", came the answer.

"May I talk with her?"

Again the small voice whispered, "No".

Knowing that it was not likely that a young child would be left home alone, the boss decided he would just leave a message with the person who should be there watching over the child. "Is there any one there besides you?" the boss asked the child.

"Yes" whispered the child, "A policeman".

Wondering what a cop would be doing at his employee's home, the boss asked, "May I speak with the policeman"?

"No, he's busy", whispered the child.

"Busy doing what?" asked the boss.

"Talking to Daddy and Mommy and the Fireman", came the whispered answer.

Growing concerned and even worried as he heard what sounded like a helicopter through the earpiece on the phone, the boss asked, "What is that noise?"

"A hello-copper", answered the whispering voice.

"What's going on there?", asked the boss, now alarmed.

In an awed whispering voice the child answered, "The search team just landed the hello-copper."

Alarmed, concerned and more than just a little frustrated, the boss asked, "Why are they there"?

Still whispering, the young voice replied along with a muffled giggle:

"They're looking for me."

Few things catch our attention in life faster than children. Their enthusiasm for living, their curiosity for learning and their openness to adventure make each day a new experience in parenting. Without a doubt, they are our greatest earthly treasure and our most prized natural resource. Their value cannot be measured.

Some of the greatest memories of your life will come from the lives of your children. They teach you to look at life from their perspective and worldview. They also force you to examine your beliefs with their relentless questions and observations. They help us see that the call to parenting remains one of the greatest, most rewarding responsibilities on the face of this earth.

At the same time, bringing children up properly can be one of the most irrational, insane and frustrating experiences of human existence. Some of the longest nights, greatest hurts and deepest pains will come from the lives of your children. Parenting is one of the most humbling responsibilities one could ever undertake. The reason is clear - there is no guaranteed formula for success. What works for one child or family may not work for another. This has compelled many parents to conclude that there are no absolutes for rearing children. In their minds, you need a lot of love and courage, along with a little luck to produce normal children.

While it's true that every child is different and that some children are harder to rear than others, it's *not* correct to conclude that no absolutes in child training exist for parents today. The Bible contains many timeless guidelines that can help parents in their responsibilities to their children. We're going to look at some of these principles as we seek to raise our abilities in child training, not our own blood pressure.

LESSON FOCUS

Once we expose the common misunderstandings about children and child-rearing as well as recognize some of the major factors that make parenting so difficult these days, we can turn to the Scriptures to learn several valuable principles that can help us "train up a child in the way he/she should go." When we understand and implement God's way of shaping children, we will learn to sow spiritual values and principles in our kid's lives that will bear fruit in good season.

COMMON MISUNDERSTANDINGS ABOUT CHILDREN AND REARING

Perhaps one of the reasons why some parents live with daily irritation over their children lies with their misconceptions about the nature of children and about their own fears in knowing how to handle them properly. Through the years, I've seen good people buckle under the task of child rearing because every child was different in their home and they didn't know how to cope. One child was sanguine while the other was phlegmatic. What's worse, another was a choleric trying to tell a melancholic how to do something. From simple observation over their dilemma, I've seen or heard a number of misconceptions and fears in their understanding of children. These perceptions help us understand why some moms and dads live with perpetual confusion in their home.

The first misconception parents have about their children is that they are blank slates. For some strange reason, a respectable number of parents actually believe that children enter life in a "neutral" position. They arrive in our world in a state of innocence. What makes a child either a good or bad person is largely determined by the environmental influences in early life. Sometime in their development, they reach "an age of accountability," where they become responsible for their actions. In essence, they are innocent until proven guilty.

The Scriptures address this issue clearly and forcefully. Nowhere are children seen or presented before God as innocent. They are sinners, guilty before God because of their rebellious nature. David wrote that he was sinful from the time his mother conceived him (Psalm 51:5). Because of their fallen human nature, humanity conceives and bears a fresh collection of iniquity into the world daily. These little people are not angels, but little sinners in diapers. The fact that the words "NO" and "MINE" form their first vocabulary words substantiate this claim. *As a parent, you must understand that your children are not neutral, but sinful.* They sin because they are sinners by birth and by practice. *You don't have to teach a child to be bad. Rather, you must continually teach him/her to be good. That's because of their sin nature.*

Another misconception that exists in the world is that good par-

ents always have good children. This misconception states that if you have a problem child, the trouble lies not with the child, but with your parenting abilities. Parents who live with heartache over their children are the ones to blame for their children's downfall. Good parents produce good kids. It's as simple as that.

I know from experience that this mindset is wrong. I have known godly men and women who have done everything possible to train their children properly. Unfortunately, their sons and daughters grew up and made the wrong decisions and followed the wrong paths in life, ruining their lives and the lives of their loved ones. *The truth of the matter is that good parents sometimes have bad kids.* Although they do everything in their power to steer their children in the right direction, they learn that these young people will decide their own destiny and fate in life. Because of this dilemma, many mothers and fathers live with daily worry over the decisions their children make.

On the other side of this perplexing situation in life comes a result that's equally confusing and misunderstood. *Sometimes the best children in the world come from the worst parental models possible.* Many of them grow up watching alcoholism absorb a parent. Others observe mom and dad argue to the point of violence while another group experiences the horror of child abuse. Yet these children grow up to be splendid models of citizenship, integrity and dependability. Perhaps their exposure to this evil compelled them to choose a different way of life when they left the home. At the same time, someone outside the home (school teacher, coach, youth pastor, scout leader) could also have modeled a meaningful way of life during their teenage years that stabilized their lives and put them on the right path before the world. In either case, the situation is clear in our world today. Good parents have bad kids and bad parents have good kids. It's hard to understand, but it's often seen.

A third misconception that parents have about child training deals with "raising over rearing." Hardly a week goes by without a parent telling me that they're doing their best to "raise" their child. So many times I've gritted my teeth and swallowed my compulsive drive to correct them on the spot. I'm sure part of the reason for my revolt against this kind of thinking stems from my agricultural background as a child. I was taught early in life that *you raise pigs, cat-*

tle and other kinds of livestock. You rear children, pulling them along in the fear and nurture of the Lord.

Some people think this issue is just a matter of semantics. I've had them tell me, "It's just a play on words." *I don't think so.* The idea of "raising" has *nothing* to do with values. By definition, it simply means supplying the food, clothing and shelter that a person needs. While this is essential in family life, it falls far short of God's requirement for bringing up children properly. Children need training, steering, discipline and focused love.[40] "Raising" doesn't include these elements in its operation. Your impact as a parent begins when you choose to rear your children, not raise them.

A fourth misconception that parents have about child rearing is that children are supposed to do what they are told to do. As a child, I remember many times when my mother or father would correct my misbehavior with these words: "Son, just do what you're told to do." I find myself now as a father of three children telling them the same thing at times; however, this form of parental influence is often ineffective. Children do not do what they hear from us; *they do what they see in us.* Parental responsibility involves proper modeling of the truth. Therefore, if you want to be an effective parent, you must model to your children the character that you want them to have.

Gordon MacDonald emphasizes how the task of modeling needs to start with the father:

> A father trains by being a model, by carefully instructing his kids on the job, by giving opportunities for his children to try it themselves. Every moment of relationship between father and children is a part of the training process. In this never-ending exercise we actually create a complex personality system of habits, reflexes, values, and ambitions.[41]

Every child deserves a good role model in life. I truly believe that the number of good role models available to our children largely determines the degree of life-changing impact that they experience.

---

[40] See Chapter 6 of Ross Campbell's work, *How to Really Love Your Child* (Victor Books, 1977).
[41] Gordon MacDonald, *The Effective Father* (Tyndale, 1977), pp. 186-187.

Young people seldom practice what they hear from a pulpit. They respond to what they see in daily life.

WHY IS CHILD REARING SO TOUGH?

James Dobson accurately describes the situation that causes so much frustration in the lives of many young mothers and fathers:

> A child between eighteen and thirty-six months of age is a sheer delight, but he can also be utterly maddening. He is inquisitive, short-tempered, demanding, cuddly, inno-cent and dangerous at the same time. I find it fascinating to watch him run through his day, seeking opportunities to crush things, flush things, kill things, spill things, fall off things, eat horrible things - and think up ways to rattle his mother. Someone said it best: The Lord made Adam from the dust of the earth, but when the first toddler came along, He added **electricity!**[42]

Maybe it's me, but it seems that the problems of our day are so much greater than the days when I was a child. Now I know that I didn't live in a fairyland in the 1960's. When I was young, the Beatles were launching a new revolution on a yellow submarine and the U.S. was heavily involved in the Vietnam War. The 1960's were a time of great cultural and social change in the world. To a great degree, we feel the effects of those former days in our current gen-eration. We see things differently than our parents and grandparents saw them. For those of us who grew up in those days and are now parents, those times affect the way we see our children and the way we think they should grow up in our world. What has the last thirty-five years produced that makes parenting an increasingly difficult dilemma?

Child rearing has become increasingly difficult due to the mobil-ity of our society. Because we're living in the greatest period of industrial, scientific and technological expansion in human history, everything is just the touch of a computer button away. With this

---

[42] James C. Dobson, *Parenting Isn't For Cowards: Dealing Confidently With the Frustra-tions of Child-Rearing* (Word, 1987), p. 20.

expansion of information and technology comes increased opportunity and mobility. People are willing to move away from family and other traditional support structures in pursuit of a better job or work that matches their technical skills. When this occurs, family and community networks are broken, separating people from one another. This situation pushes parents to the brink because it makes them feel that they're all alone in the responsibilities of child rearing. In the past, grandmothers, grandfathers, aunts, uncles and other family members lived close to your home. They had an important influencing role upon children in their formative years. Now that families are hundreds, even thousands of miles apart these days, it's hard to get help in steering children through the stages of their lives.

A friend of mine who worked for International Business Machines once told me that another name for IBM was "I've been moved." Judging from his attitude, I knew there was a great deal of bitterness over the way businesses like to uproot people and to send them to another office. *But no one does it better than the military.* They love to move people at the snap of a finger. I've pastored in a military town, so I've watched this up close and personal. I know the military's top brass say it must be done "for the sake of freedom," but I question a respectable portion of it. You feel the hurt when families have to move. I've heard their pain when they call after their move and say that they're spiritually starving in their new community because there isn't a good church community nearby. Families with children need stability and security in their surroundings. When this stability is threatened, additional tensions and stresses come into the home not only on the parents, but also on the children.

Another reason why child rearing is increasingly difficult in our day is due to the erosion of moral values in our culture. Our generation continues to reap the results of an age where wrong is elevated as right and right is demoted as wrong. Postmodernism has brainwashed the minds of our children and youth to the point that many believe that premarital sex is fun, safe and fulfilling. Relativism presents homosexuality and lesbianism as legitimate lifestyles. More children than we can count are spoon-fed the tenets of secular humanism in our schools daily. They're led to believe that evolution is true science and that man is a product of chance over billions of years, having no sacred dignity or value before God. Many

Christian historians tell us that the problems of our age have come because the church failed to preach loudly the reality of sin and the importance of absolute truth in the early to middle part of this century. Because of this silence, society is getting worse. There is continual erosion of truth and moral values in our time.

This disintegration of values and morality has come largely from the influence of television over our children. You get the idea that Hollywood knows what your children need more than you do. Because of this, parents find themselves wrestling with their children over conflicting values presented by the major networks. Television has done more to change the course of values and ethics than any other instrument in human history. When you add to this problem the immense pressure our children receive from peers to adopt these Hollywood principles of morality, you find the potential for a new civil war developing within your home. The problems of depravity and humanism make child rearing overwhelming at times.

This problem of sin and humanism produces another reason for current day child rearing difficulties. When you add conflicting moral values to the depravity that comes from sin, you see the adolescent struggle for power rise in the home. It seems that every family has at least one child who seeks to control the whole household, including the parents. These power lords, called strong-willed children, require constant supervision, threats and other warnings to keep their behavior in line. When these children enter the family, the home becomes a tactical base for strategic battle and conflict. In their minds they want to control and to win over authority.

In his book, *Parenting Isn't For Cowards*, James Dobson presents this dilemma of control in the home as a "power game."[43] In this contest, children attempt to challenge their parents' authority by failing to work with them over areas where cooperation is needed. Homework, bedtime, TV, food and vacations are several areas in the family where these power plays are most likely to occur. Left unchecked, these struggles can turn into modern day Gettysburgs in the home. Rearing a strong-willed child remains a major battleground in modern day parenting. When you have a couple of them

---

[43] *Parenting Isn't For Cowards*, p. 109.

in the house, look out! Storms are coming!

A fourth reason why parenting is so difficult for moms and dads today comes from their own doubt, inadequacy and fears about child rearing. They confess an inability to know the right things to guide their children in the right direction. Too many times, they throw their hands up in the air, crying for help and wisdom in times of indecision. Because of this doubt, far too many parents live with feelings of failure in their lives. Sometimes these moments of doubt and failure produce periods of deep depression and self-condemnation. I've heard parents say, "I don't know what to do with this child!" Their frustrating cries ring loud and clear with doubt and disappointment. Can you identify?

God has provided hope and help for parents who find child rearing unbearable. In addition to the inner wisdom He provides (James 1:5), God also gives us His written Word which is a lamp to our feet and a light to our path (Psalm 119:105). He also provides older men and women with advice and experience (Proverbs 11:14). These and other resources are available to you when you struggle with indecision and uncertainty in your role as a parent. Much of it starts with a proper understanding of Proverbs 22:6. When you begin to see the meaning of this verse in light of the children in your home, you'll sense a greater confidence in fulfilling your God-given role as a parent.

THE MEANING OF PROVERBS 22:6

Solomon wrote, "Train up a child in the way he should go, and when he is old he will not turn from it" (Proverbs 22:6). This verse supplies several important principles and implications that are necessary for effective child rearing. The key to discovering these principles involves a proper understanding of the text in the light of Jewish culture.

The crux of this verse centers in the phrase "in the way he should go." What does this "way" mean? For many years, I thought this passage meant that the focus of child training involved instilling in your children the moral values that they *need* to know in order to stay on the "straight and narrow path." I thought it meant that if you taught your children the Ten Commandments and the essentials of the gospel message, they would return to the Law of God for the rest of their life after their years of teenage rebellion. But upon closer study of this verse, I came to see that the passage doesn't support this traditional opinion. A closer examination of this phrase "in the way he should go" was needed.

This Hebrew phrase can better be translated, "in the way of his going." In other words, we need to train up children in ways that correspond closely to their nature, personality and interests in life. Frank Delitzsch writes:

> The instruction of youth, the education of youth, ought to be conformed to the nature of youth; the matter of instruction, the manner of instruction, ought to regulate itself according to the stage of life, and its peculiarities; the method ought to be arranged according to the degree of development which the mental and bodily life of the youth has arrived at.[44]

When I came to understand that training and mentoring should closely parallel a child's personality, stage in life, interests and development, it made me appreciate something critically important in parenting; something I wish I knew in the days when I was a father of my young children. Child rearing has everything to do with *direct involvement in the daily life of your child.* Delitzsch's insight helps us uncover three important principles that can guide us in the kind of child rearing that pleases God.

Observe Interests

Solomon intended for parents to train their children in the things that interested them. This means that children who show a curiosity for science should receive special attention in science. Those who show interest in agriculture should receive direction in agriculture. Those who like music should be sent to music instructors. In other words, *parents should set the agenda for their children's education based on their observations about the child's interests in life.* Of

---

[44] Frank Delitzsch, *Commentary on The Old Testament: Volume VI: Proverbs, Ecclesiastes, Song of Solomon* (Eerdmans, 1978), pp. 86-87.

course children receive general training in all fields of knowledge, but in addition to this, they should be directed to pursue the special fields of education that interest them. With this in mind, Solomon instructs parents to watch their children closely to see the legitimate things of life that catch their time and attention. Good child rearing involves knowing the interests of your children and guiding them to pursue their interests with proper training and oversight.

When our children were in their preschool years, dinosaurs fascinated them. So our family took a Spring Break trip to the Smithsonian in Washington, DC, to see the dinosaurs in the Museum of Natural Science and History. Then as they grew, airplanes became the big topic of observation and study. So we made regular visits to the airport to see the big planes take off and land. After that, baseball and softball excited their interest, so my wife and I bought some gloves and bats and spent regular times in the back yard teaching them how to throw, hit and catch properly. It paid off! All of them did well and enjoy playing! *The key is observation.* Look closely at the things that attract their attention. If it's music, encourage it. If it's reading, put a book in their hands. When you see something that interests them, encourage them in that direction.

INTENTIONAL LEARNING IN THE FIELD

Once a child demonstrated an interest in a particular field of learning, the parents should then seek to train their child in the rigors of that skill. The child in carpentry school should practice the skills of measuring, cutting and sanding wood. The young lad in poetry school should practice the essential skills of creative writing, grammar and sentence structure. If a child showed interest and ability in music, they should be tutored in music. While this critical stage of education takes place, the parents should encourage their child to stretch his/her mind to the fullest so that they can master the subject. When finished with their formal schooling, that child will have specific skills to earn a living based on their curiosity and interest, not on their parent's preference. Therefore they will make a living out of the things that they *enjoy* doing, not just the things that others *think* they should do.

With this in mind, think of your own children. What interests do they have? Is someone interested in music? Are you encouraging them to play an instrument? Is anyone interested in fixing cars? By all means, we need good car repairmen these days! Have you encouraged them to visit an automobile shop? Do you have a child who loves to plant flowers and shrubs? Have you tried to connect them with a landscape designer or a nursery owner? The key is finding people or resources that match your child's interest and connecting them to one another *intentionally*. Sometimes it will work. Other times you and your child will discover that this is NOT the field that they thought it would be. When this happens, you move on and look for something else.

GO WITH THE FLOW

Obviously, there will come times in a child's training process when he/she loses heart in the field of study. In this case, "go with the flow." You need to be patient with your children, realizing that it's *their* lives and *their* interests that made them choose a specific course of study, not your preference. At the same time, remember that you need to instill discipline to build the character qualities that will help them later in life. Training up a child in the way of his going means flexibility and persistence in your life. Effective child rearing involves an appreciation for the interests of your children along with a discipline that motivates them to complete their training in a way that prepares them for life. So start looking at your children from this point of view. Watch their interests. Encourage intentional learning. Go with the flow with them as they learn. And while all of this is going on, instill biblical values in their heart.

STARTING BIBLICAL PRINCIPLES FOR EFFECTIVE PARENTING

I've learned from experience that there is no guaranteed "magic wand" formula for successful child rearing. I've heard successful parents talk about something that worked for them that *didn't* work for another family. Perhaps you've picked up the hottest book on the subject and have become discouraged, even depressed over the things you tried to do for your children. Bringing up children in our day isn't easy. Therefore it's important to start *with God at the cen-*

ter. This means you recognize that you're in a state of inadequacy and inability at the beginning. It is in this position that the God can use you as an effective parent if you will let Him. *Complete dependence on the Holy Spirit is the foundation for meaningful child rearing in our day.* If you trust Him, God can and will do things through you to impact your children.

With this in mind, there are several biblical principles that can guide you in your task of training, rearing and impacting your children. The first principle involves your relationship with your spouse.

You start to become an effective parent when you love your spouse. Someone once told a group of fathers that the *best* way they can love their children is to love their children's mother *first*. The loving, romantic and committed "till death do us part" bond between a father and mother is an essential element in bringing up healthy, normal kids. Children need to see and to sense the stability and strength of a lasting love between their mother and a father. This kind of love points them to God. It shows them that the Lord intended for humanity to live with order, peace and contentment in life.

As I write this, I realize that this situation doesn't describe many homes today. For many children, the father or the mother is not at home because of death, divorce or separation. We're living in a day where more than half of all marriages ends up in divorce. Too many children have only one parent or grandparent bringing them up in their formative years. If this describes you, you need to ask God in prayer to place around your children stable believers from solid marriages and homes who will evidence this truth and be good role models. Broken homes need the church now more than ever before to model the love of God through meaningful relationships. It is in these intentional relationships that stability and self-worth appears. Children are attracted to fathers and mothers who love each other. Their love for one another points them to the love that God has for them.

Another important ingredient in effective parenting is prayer. As parents, we need to present our children before the throne of God to ask Him to penetrate their lives with His presence, truth, love and mercy. Prayer is the only thing that can produce meaningful change in anyone's heart, whether the child is young or grownup. It's God's instrument for permanent behavior adjustment.

Prayer not only changes the lives of children, but our lives, too. When we pray, we understand God's view of our children. We see how valuable they are in the sight of the Lord. We receive God's guidance in parenting. The Holy Spirit speaks to us with a still small voice, reminding us how He treats us as His children so that we may understand our children properly. Without a doubt, a praying parent is an effective parent in the sight of God. Without prayer, we lose our perspective in child rearing.

This principle came to life for me when my second child was saying her prayers one night when she was four years old. As she was talking to God, she asked him to bless the usual things in her life—our family, both grandmas, all her aunts, uncles, cousins and friends along with our own dog and cat. When she finished her usual list, I could tell that she couldn't think of anything else for which to thank God. She stuttered a bit, trying to muster up something else to thank God for in her life. Finally, she stopped, grabbed her composure and said, "GOD, I JUST WANT YOU TO KNOW THAT YOU'RE GREAT!" As I heard this, my heart leaped. Little daughter taught daddy a mighty big lesson on prayer that night!

Another effective principle in child rearing is to model God's love through affirmation. Psalm 103:13 reminds us, "As a father has compassion on his children, so the Lord has compassion on those who fear Him." This verse teaches us that parents need to demonstrate to their children the compassion, grace and kindness that God demonstrates in their lives. Parents need to model this love so that their children grow up in an atmosphere of acceptance and significance. Children need to know daily that God loves them; they understand this through their parents' love for them.

I'm discovering that many parents find it difficult to express love to their children. Perhaps when these parents were children, no one regularly hugged, kissed or affirmed their worth in a positive way. This difficulty needs overcoming. Affectionate love, expressed in appropriate ways, speaks loudly to children. Not only does it communicate self-worth, but also it keeps children from deviating into sexual disorientation later in life. Ross Campbell wrote, "In all my reading and experience, I have never known of one sexually disoriented person who had a warm, loving and affectionate father.[45] Effective child rearing produces an affectionate, affirming love to children, giving them a proper perspective of God.

Another significant resource in effective child rearing is the appropriate use of discipline. Hebrews 12:5-7 reminds us of the importance of God's discipline in our lives: "My son, do not make light of the Lord's discipline, and do not lose heart when he rebukes you, because the Lord disciplines those he loves, and he punishes everyone he accepts as a son. Endure hardship as discipline; God is treating you as sons. For what son is not disciplined by his father?"

We learn from Scripture that discipline is essential in child rearing. Children need parents who will steer them in the right direction, correcting them when they go astray and instructing them when they do wrong. Failure to use appropriate discipline in a child's life opens the door to weakness and instability.

It seems that in our day of civil rights, personal freedom, self-expression and permissiveness, discipline has received bad publicity. Bruce Ray reminds us that this spirit is a trademark of evil:

> Is it any wonder, then, that the same educators have found it necessary in many of our great cities to man the halls of the schools with police armed with pistols, night sticks, mace, and tear gas? Is it any wonder that in the suburbs of our land mothers are afraid to send their children to school, lest they be assaulted between classes or even in the midst of a class? Is it any wonder that in the schools of our land teachers fear for their very lives, lest they be beaten or even **killed** by their students? Is it any wonder that the school districts complain year after year and spend increasingly more of our money to replace chemistry labs that have been purposely destroyed, to replace broken windows and repair other acts of vandalism, when we encourage children to express their sinful selves? Permissiveness is not the strategy of the Scriptures: it is

---

[45] Ross Campbell, *How to Really Love Your Child*, p. 73.
[46] Bruce A. Ray, *Withhold Not Correction* (Presbyterian and Reformed Publishing Company, 1978), p. 31.

the strategy of the devil.[46]

Proverbs 22:15 tells us, *"Folly is bound up in the heart of a child, but the rod of discipline will drive it far from him."* Appropriate correction at the right time can make child rearing a positive experience in the life of a child as well as a parent.[47]

Another effective tool in successful parenting that I want to highlight is what's often called the "spontaneous moment." This principle addresses those parents who experience frustration over unsuccessful attempts to have a family devotion time. It seems often that when some families come together to read the Bible or to pray, something happens to cause distraction. The phone rings, the dog barks, the doorbell sounds, the baby cries or one of the children misbehaves. I know in my own life how meaningless family devotions were at times. My mother tried her best to make it work, but the chemistry and timing failed to appear. We grumbled at the mention of family devotions. The reason was simple. This form of togetherness was an unnatural way to interject meaning and value in family life.

Don't misunderstand me at this point. I'm *not* saying that family prayer time and Bible reading is unimportant. If your family has these kinds of devotions and it's working, keep it up! But I'm finding from scores of families that this practice is more frustrating than rewarding. Something is needed to interject biblical truths in a realistic, natural setting.

Deuteronomy 6 sheds some light for seeing effective child rearing in a family setting. Moses told the mothers and fathers of the land to impress God's commandments into their children's lives not in a lecture setting, but in a spontaneous setting: *"These commandments that I give you today are to be upon your hearts. Impress them on your children. Talk about them when you sit at home and when you walk along the road, when you lie down and when you get up* (6:6-7).

I think this spontaneous interjection of biblical truths comes best in the natural situations of life. Family fun activities, sporting

---

[47] So much could be said about this subject, so please refer to *Shepherding a Child's Heart* by Ted Tripp for more helpful discussion on the manner and motives of child discipline.

events, work projects, crisis situations and vacations create the greatest opportunities for parents to train children in the ways of God. The key to impacting your children involves knowing those "golden" moments when they're open to hearing our truths and values in a natural way. When you're alert to the opportunities for biblical spontaneous interjection, the Holy Spirit can impact your children with life-changing power.

These principles of child rearing, based in complete dependence upon the Holy Spirit, form an effective method of training and nurturing children to fear the Lord. Without a doubt, there will be times of frustration and discouragement in parenting. But at the same time, there will come great rewards and benefits for rearing children in a way that honors God.

THE REWARDS OF EFFECTIVE CHILD REARING

I want to conclude by looking at something that can encourage all of us who are rearing children today. These are the rewards that come from parenting in the way of the Lord. Proverbs 23:24-25 teaches us, *"The father of a righteous man has great joy; he who has a wise son delights in him. May your father and mother be glad; may she who gave you birth rejoice!"* Nothing brings greater joy and longer fulfillment in life than to watch a child grow up to embrace the person of Christ and to make a lasting contribution to society. There's no doubt that parenting is difficult, but so very rewarding in at least two special ways.

The first way it's rewarding is from the memories it brings to your life. Proper time, training and togetherness will produce some of your most cherished family memories. Vacations traveled, birthday parties enjoyed, holiday times together, school projects completed and lessons learned along the way form the greatest memories that will ever come to a family. Effective parenting produces lasting memories that will never go away.

As my children have grown through the years, it's amazing to me when I see them regularly pulling out the old family VCR videos that I made when they did their school plays, ball games, birthday parties and Christmas Day gatherings around the tree. Those memories never fade. They only *increase* as they grow older in life. The positive, loving things you do as a parent when they're young produce good fruit in the years to come.

Steven Bly, in his book, *How to be a Good Dad*, shows how good fathers make good memories in the lives of their children:

> You added much to their lives when they were tiny. When they got scared, it was your hand they clutched. When they couldn't see the parade, it was your shoulders they sat on. When they wanted an ice cream cone, it was your pocket they tugged. When they scratched their knee, it was your lap they cried in. When they built a house of blocks, they sought out your approval. When the neighbor kids didn't treat them right, it was your hug they wanted. When they struck out at the baseball game, it was your eyes they tried to avoid. When they learned the new trick on the bike, it was you they wanted to impress. When they received honors at school, you were the first to see the trophy. When they met the perfect girl or guy, you were the important one to get introduced. When they got the promotion at work, you were the first person they called. The reason's simple. You're their daddy - you always have been and always will be.[48]

No one can remove the lasting memories formed by good parenting. They create an imperishable reward.

The second way parenting is rewarding is from the heritage it produces for generations to come. Solomon wrote about the legacy that comes from rearing children in the way of the Lord: "Sons are a heritage from the Lord, children a reward from him. Like arrows in the hands of a warrior are sons born in one's youth. Blessed is the man whose quiver is full of them" (Psalm 127:3-5a).

Effective child rearing will produce generations of young people who will shine like bright lights in a dark and decaying world. The children we train to fear and love God will be future parents who will instruct the next generation to walk in the Lord's ways. The dif-

---

[48] Steven A. Bly, *How to be a Good Dad* (Moody, 1986), pp. 128-129.

ference starts when we commit ourselves *now* to do the best job we can as parents, depending on God's Spirit to lead the way.

SUMMARY

There are many misconceptions that people have about parenting in the world today. Children aren't blank slates. They are born with a sin nature and must be evangelized, nurtured and trained in the fear and admonition of the Lord through prayer, appropriate discipline, affirmative love and encouragement. Proverbs 22:6 teaches us to observe our child's interests and to encourage pursuit of those interests through training and skill development. When we do this, they stand a better chance of becoming productive citizens in their community. Effective parenting starts with love in the home—love for your spouse, then love for your child. Enjoy them while they're under your roof. Understand the legacy that they represent and do everything you can to rear them appropriately. But understand something clearly—*TIME IS SHORT*. You only have them for a short window of time. Invest yourself in them as much as you possibly can *now*. One day they'll leave your home and be on their own. Until that happens, give all you can to mold them into something special in God's sight. After all, they are the only lasting treasures that you can take to heaven with you from this earth.

REFLECTION

So many memories flood my mind when I reflect back to the days when our three children were small. I'm grateful that our VCR camcorder recorded many of these unforgettable moments. In fact, my girls get some of these tapes out and play them once in a while. Many of them are funny and could only be enjoyed within the family. But there's one event that comes to my mind involving my son and me that I'll never forget. The camcorder wasn't handy at the time, but thankfully two men nearby had a camera and took several pictures that will never leave our family scrapbook.

When my son was between four and five years old, I decided to take him on his first official fishing trip. It was a chilly, blustery March afternoon that required a seasonal jacket to stay comfortable in the elements. My son dressed for the occasion, wearing his farmer's overalls, striped colored t-shirt, scuffed sneakers and red mesh St. Louis baseball cap. He was excited and ready to catch his first fish. As we got out of the car, he kept saying, "Daddy, God's gonna give me a fish!" I smiled and held his hand as we walked to the pond together.

This was no ordinary pond. It was a special place owned by my now departed friend who was as close to me as a spiritual brother could get. In his cozy cabin, dozens of pictures hung on the wall near the dining table that spotlighted numerous father-son hunting and fishing expeditions on his property in the past. Near the fireplace were numerous wildlife busts—deer, turkey, bobcat and other animals I couldn't identify. You name it and it was probably on display in the cabin.

My son was trying out his new fishing pole that day. It was the one that had his favorite cartoon character on the reel attached to a child-sized rod. He was so proud of it as we walked to the spot where I had caught some big fish in the past. All around my friend's property were scores of wildlife. We saw three deer near the old tractor barn and heard several turkeys in the distance. The pond contained some of the biggest bass you'll ever catch. We weren't just going to fish "somewhere." In my mind, we were on special ground.

When we reached the shore, I started to show my boy some of the finer sides of fishing—digging the worm out of the box, sticking the hook in it and positioning the cork on the line so that the bait was at the proper depth. His look at that squirming worm made me think I had lost him for a moment! But after I explained to him that this wiggling was a *dance* that worms used to entertain fish, he accepted it. We tossed the line in the water and waited for the fish to strike.

Nothing happened. Remember, it was a chilly, windy March day in Alabama and fish simply don't eat. Minutes turned into an hour. Nothing moved. We didn't even get a *nibble*. The east wind sent ripples across the surface of the pond and I started to get worried. There was no hope of catching anything. Would my son lose interest? Would he give up fishing after one try? The longer we watched, the more anxious I became.

For the first hour, the lack of action didn't seem to bother my son. He was glad to be outside having some "daddy time." The birds and wildlife sounds intrigued him. But I could tell he wanted to catch a fish; however the pond wasn't cooperating. We changed baits, walked around the water to different stop points, raised and lowered the cork, but nothing happened, not even a look of interest from a fish. But that didn't disturb him from believing that he'd get a fish. He kept telling me, "Daddy, God's gonna give me a fish!" I smiled and told him, "Son, he'll find a way. He always does!"

When all hope seemed gone, two friends in my church who were fishing out in a boat on the other side of the pond rowed near us and asked how we were doing. With a "thumbs down" sign, I looked at Mike and Bill and said, "We can't get a bite!"

Then it happened.

Mike looked at me and lip-synced, "toss me his line and distract his attention for a moment. We'll hook one of our big bream on it and throw it back in the water."

I couldn't believe this stroke of opportunity. And I went along with it! In less than a minute, Mike and Bill put a beautiful three quarter pound bream on my son's hook, tossed it in the water, rowed away from the cork, and then signaled to me that the coast was clear.

I turned my boy around and said, "Son, I've gotta a good feeling that something's gonna happen! Look at your cork! Keep looking!"

For the first ten seconds, the cork didn't move. I began to wonder if the fish was dead or if it escaped the hook. Those seconds seemed like eternity. But suddenly, the cork went down and I yelled, "SON, PULL!"

With all the strength and excitement that a preschool boy could muster, he reeled that bream in on his toy fishing pole and looked at it with awe and amazement. Mike and Bill pulled their boat close to the shore and took a couple of pictures that humbly serve as the witness of this "tall fish tale."

But what hit me the most was the words my son said as he looked at his prized catch.

"Daddy, I told you. I told you it would happen."

"What, son? What would happen?"

"I told you that God would give me a fish. *He didn't let me down.*"

"You're right, pal. He doesn't disappoint. He's always faithful."

And we called it a day and went home.

PRAYER

Heavenly Father, next to my eternal life and my spouse, you've given me the greatest treasure in the world in the lives of my children. Thank you for the joy in life that they bring as well as the challenges and difficulties they give to living at times. Today, I'm committing myself to becoming a more effective parent in their lives. Help me to love my spouse today in such a way that they feel the stability of committed love. Give me the power to show affirming love to them as I counsel, direct and steer them in the ways of Christ. Give me wisdom to see their interests in life and to help them learn the way of their going. Dear Lord, build me children who are strong in the grace of God and walk in courage with the faith that is given them from You. Use me by Your grace to create a lasting memory and heritage in their life. For the glory of Christ our King, I pray. AMEN.

TALK TIME!

1. What misconceptions about parenting have you heard in the world? What false ideas about rearing children were revealed to you after you became a parent?
2. As your children grow older, what do they teach you about child rearing?
3. Look over some of the reasons why parenting is so tough these days. Which one is hardest on you? Can you add other reasons?
4. Review the basic principles for effective child rearing. Which one do you feel you need to work on the most? How will you work on it?
5. Take some time to discuss discipline. Is this easy or hard for you to do?
6. How can "spontaneous interjection" of biblical values help you look for the "golden" moments?
7. When all is said and done, what do you want your children to remember about you as a parent?
8. Do you know someone who needs some help and guidance in parenting their children? How can this lesson equip you to help him/her?

12

I Owe, I Owe,
It's Off to Work I Go

*"Let no debt remain outstanding, except the continuing debt to
love one another, for he who loves his fellow man
has fulfilled the law."*
Romans 13:8

I knew something was wrong the moment I picked up the phone. I could hardly voice a traditional "hello" before the sniffles and sounds of brokenness flooded the airwaves of the phone. "Pastor," she said, "I'm in big trouble." She wasn't a frequent phone caller, so I knew this was important. And the longer she talked, the more her speech crumbled. She was deeply hurt and crying out for help.

I asked her to calm down and to tell me what was disturbing her. She told me that earlier in the day, a credit manager from a large local department store called about their delinquent bill. Several months ago, they purchased a new refrigerator and a home entertainment system for their apartment. They used store credit, committing to pay it off in 36 monthly installments. Three months later, no payment was received. The credit manager called with some nasty, threatening words. She took them personally.

If pain and anguish could travel through telephone lines, you could feel it with this call. From the sound of her voice, I knew she had cried for several hours. She explained to me her husband's rationale for the home theatre system and her need for a new refrigerator. "It looked so good on the showroom floor, but now the shine has gone," she said. For weeks to come, she lived with sleepless nights, carrying the burden of a debt that they couldn't pay.

Practically everything looks and sounds good on display. It's clean. It sparkles under the lights. It works and looks just right. It penetrates you just like the look of the puppy dog in the pet store picture window. It begs you to take it home for a price.

You take the plunge. They debit your account. You get it home. That day, there's no greater priority than to open the box and to read the installation instructions. You finish hooking it up and then it goes on. It works fine and you sit down in your favorite chair. A check mark goes on your mental want list as you sit in accomplished satisfaction. Then after the glamour of the product fades, the first bill arrives. And the downhill spiral starts as you realize *you have just sold yourself to a form of modern day slavery.*

During part of his adult life, Mark Twain was bankrupt. He made money when he wrote books. However when he chose publishing instead of writing, he fell into financial trouble. So he went back to writing and to the lecture circuit, erasing all his debts with his new works. But in the process of doing this, he formulated a strong opinion about the banking business in his time.

He called a banker in his day, "a fellow who lends you his umbrella when the sun is shining and wants it back the minute it begins to rain."[50] You may have heard his invented story of a bank president who was proud of a glass eye that a famous Paris artist made for him. He said, "Twain, you need $5,000.00. I'll give it to you if you can guess which of my eyes is the glass one." Twain quickly snapped, "It's the left one, of course. It's the only one with a glint of human kindness in it."[51]

I'm not against bank presidents. I've known a few of them in my time and have found them to be fine, reputable people. The issue here is deeper than a person in a bank office. It's a problem plaguing hundreds of thousands of people today. It's called debt.

Everyday, more people go into the world and spend more money than they make. When this happens, they put themselves in grave danger. In effect, they're selling their soul to future slavery for

[50] Attributed to Twain. Found at www.geocities.com/gunjansaraf/twain.htm
[51] Paul Lee Tan, *Encyclopedia of 7700 Illustrations* (Assurance Publishers, 1979), p. 317-318.

immediate satisfaction. They remind me of the old German proverb that says, "He who borrows sells his freedom." I know many people living under that kind of bondage today. Are you one of them? How did you get that way? Can you find a way out? Is there really hope? What does the Bible have to say about this? Where's God when you're head over heels in debt?

WHY ARE MONEY AND POSSESSIONS SIGNIFICANT TO GOD?

Several trusted Bible teachers compiled and studied all the verses in the Scriptures attributed to Jesus on a number of subjects. Their conclusions may surprise you when it comes to this issue. When they examined all the recorded words of Jesus, *a full 15% dealt in some way with money and possessions.*[52] That's far more than prayer, faith, heaven or hell. What's the point? Why does Christ spend so much time telling us about money and possessions or the lack thereof?

Jesus wouldn't have spent a great deal of time on this subject without a reason. Therefore, it's important that we gain a biblical understanding about money and the proper way to handle it. After all, He doesn't want you living in bondage. He wants you to chart your life course on the road to freedom today. But for this to happen, you must understand some important principles about money and possessions and their role in God's eternal perspective for your life.

First, your perspective on money and possessions reveals a lot about your worldview. A person's attitude and use of money reveals their outlook on life. Zacchaeus represents a good example of this principle. In Luke 19 we learn that Jesus met this wealthy, chief tax collector in Jericho. Because of his small stature, he couldn't see the Lord. So he climbed a sycamore tree. Jesus saw him, told him to come down and asked to go to Zacchaeus' house. While people in the crowd looked at this action with disgust, Zacchaeus told the Lord a startling action. He announced that half of his possessions would go to the poor and that he would pay back four times the

---

[52] Randy Alcorn, *Money, Possessions and Eternity* (Tyndale, 1989), p. 17.

amount to anyone he had cheated.

Look at Jesus' words in verse 9, "Today salvation has come to this house, because this man, too is a son of Abraham." *Christ used Zacchaeus' words to show the value of the eternal through the distribution of the physical.* Zacchaeus' mind was not concerned with earthly things. His actions reveal a worldview that was focused on heavenly things.

This principle compels me to ask you some thought-provoking questions. How do you view your possessions? How do you see your bank account(s)? Do they exist to honor God or to satisfy your personal agenda? Do you love to make money for what it does to you or do you love to make money for the effect it has on God's Kingdom? The answers to these questions greatly reveal your worldview about money and possessions.

Second, your perspective on money and possessions reveals a lot about your priorities in life. Your attitude and use of money and things tell others what you think is important in this world. They show what you value and pursue in everyday life. If it's important for you to have that luxury boat, you'll find ways to make extra money to buy it. If you want your child(ren) to have the best education available in your town, you'll either find a home in the neighborhood zoned for the best school or you'll bite the bullet and pay tuition for private school education. *If something is valuable to you, you'll do whatever it takes to get it.* That's the reality about priorities. It's been around as long as humans have lived on this planet.

A good biblical example of this principle is the rich young ruler in Matthew 19. He came to the Lord and asked Him in verse 16, *"Teacher, what good thing must I do to get eternal life?"* Jesus replied by telling him to obey the commandments. The young ruler looked back at him and boasted that he has kept all of them throughout his life. Was something else needed? Jesus penetrated to the heart issue of this man's life. He answered, *"If you want to be perfect, go, sell your possessions and give to the poor, and you will have treasure in heaven. Then come, follow me"* (19:21). We see that upon hearing this, the rich man went away sad. His earthly treasures represented a priority in his life.

Jesus used this incident as a springboard to launch into a discussion about salvation. In His mind, if you have the priorities of the rich young ruler, it's hard to enter the Kingdom of Heaven. Why? Because in this man's case, *the pursuit of riches showed a human-centered priority to find peace and security apart from God.* If your priority in life is to build wealth at all cost, you'll become human-centered rather than God-centered. You will set your desire on physical and worldly things, not on eternal and heavenly things. You'll look to the physical to satisfy the emotional and spiritual dimensions of your life.

Does this mean that there will be none of earth's wealthy people in heaven? Of course not! Jesus knew that people would ask this question, so he gave an illustration to clarify his teaching in the following verses. He used the common household sewing needle[53] and a camel to teach that it's hard, even impossible, for a rich man to enter the Kingdom of Heaven (19:24). Why? *Because salvation is a work of God, not of humanity.* You can't buy heaven with wealth or your own actions. Heaven is a free gift, given by God's grace (Ephesians 2:8-9). Jesus knew the rich young ruler wanted to buy his way into the Kingdom of God. *He wanted to take worldly resources to purchase eternal realities.* In God's plan, that was unattainable. That's why Christ told His disciples in verse 26, *"with man this is impossible, but with God all things are possible."* The attitude and value you give to money and to earthly possessions reveals the priority that you give to Christ and to His eternal Kingdom.

Third, your perspective on money and possessions reveals a lot about the depth of your spiritual life. If someone looked at your monthly expenditures, would they see a deep love for Christ and His church? If people came into your home or rode in your car, could they detect the value you place upon the things that God values in this world (peace, family values, love, etc.)? *Keep in mind that money and possessions are simply instruments. They have no intrinsic moral value in themselves;* however, they allow others to perceive what you believe is valuable in this world.

You may be thinking that I'm inferring that if you're a Christian, you *must* live in a below middle-class home or drive a sub-par car

---

[53] "Needle in Jesus' day means the same thing in our day. It didn't mean a small gate in the city for a bare back camel to pass. See Craig S. Keener, *The IVP Bible Background Commentary* (IVP, 1993), p. 98.

in order to be a good witness. *I'm not saying this at all.* This principle has little to do with the size of your home or car or the neighborhood in which it's located. I've been in the homes of some very rich people where you can sense the peace of Christ and the love that flows from one family member to another. At the same time, I've also visited people who live in the flats of public housing projects and detected a bitter, jealous spirit among the residents. I've also seen reverse scenarios, too. Some wealthy homes ooze materialism while some poorer homes evidence faith, hope and love. I say it again: *Money, possessions and physical things have no intrinsic moral values. They're simply instruments that allow people the opportunity to look into the window of your soul.*

Two contrasting gospel accounts teach this principle clearly. The first account comes from the actions of the poor widow in Mark 12:41-44. While many placed large offerings into the temple treasury, she deposited two insignificant copper coins into the collection receptacles. Jesus saw this action and commended the faith of this peasant to His disciples. Notice how He elevated her spiritual example: *"This poor widow has put more into the treasury than all the others. They all gave out of their wealth; but she, out of her poverty, put in everything—all she had to live on"* (43-44). This woman understood that God would supply all her needs from the riches and glories found only in Christ (Philippians 4:19). Her actions reveal a depth of trust and commitment to God and to His daily care of her life. You could see the depth of her spiritual walk with God.

Another account that illustrates this principle is seen in Luke 12. Beginning in verse 16, Jesus told a parable to show how greed can destroy a person's spiritual life. In this true-to-life story, a farmer decides to tear down his barns and to build bigger ones to stockpile his crops for personal gain and worldly security. Verse 19 records his attitude quite clearly: *"You have plenty of good things laid up for many years. Take life easy; eat, drink and be merry."* At first glance, one could look at this and say, "What's wrong with this? Is it sinful to accumulate? Can't I enjoy some of the fruit of my hard labors? Is it wrong to possess more? Can I gain a legitimate profit?"

I believe the issue in this parable is not about accumulation. It's about greed. This man wanted to pursue his selfish ways with little concern for the welfare of others. He had a shallow spiritual life. He wanted to trust in himself rather than in God. Because of this, Jesus says in verse 20, *"You fool! This very night your life will be demanded from you. Then who will get what you have prepared for yourself? This is how it will be with anyone who stores up things for himself but is not rich toward God."* Your attitude toward money and possessions shows the depth of your spiritual life. You can be worldly rich and eternally rich toward God. You can be worldly poor and eternally poor toward God and every other option in-between. It's a matter of daily choices.

Fourth, your perspective on money and possessions reveals a lot about the focus and passions in your life. Although they may not show what you currently have, they can uncover the things in life that you're pursuing with determination. If your focus is to join the country club at all costs so that you'll gain the social status that you crave, you'll pursue it with daily passion; however, if your focus in joining the country club is to make regular contacts with people so that you can share the gospel with them, your daily motives will be quite different. The key word here is *motives.* Why do you pursue the things you do? What is the intent behind your daily actions?

An illustration of this principle is the woman with expensive perfume in Mark 14. While Jesus was staying at the home of Simon the Leper in Bethany, a woman came and broke an alabaster jar of costly perfume and poured it on His head. While some gave indignant looks, others rebuked her actions because of the value of the perfume and its use in that setting. But Jesus commended this woman's passion with approving words. From God's perspective, she poured perfume to prepare Jesus' body for burial; therefore Christ honored her sacrifice and passion by saying these words, *"I tell you the truth, wherever the gospel is preached throughout the world, what she has done will also be told in memory of her"* (14:9). This jar of perfume was probably the most expensive earthly possession that she had. But her passion for Christ turned it into a gift to share. Through her we see that a person's attitude toward money and possessions reveals the passions in life.

With this in mind, think of the things that you're pursuing these days. Why are you focused on them? Do you buy a car for status or for dependable, safe transportation? Do you buy a house to honor

God and to meet the specific needs of your family or do you pursue size and luxury as a status symbol? In many respects, the pursuit of money and possessions is like a spiritual barometer in our life. You can learn a lot about a person's worldview and passions by looking at their life pursuits. This explains why many people go into credit card and consumer debt.

WHY DO PEOPLE GO INTO CREDIT CARD AND CONSUMER DEBT?

It's time to address an issue that is often discussed in church circles and on Christian radio. It's about borrowing and going into debt. Is any kind of borrowing wrong? Does the Bible *prohibit every form* of debt? The answer is *NO!* There are *legitimate times* when people need to borrow money. You need to see that the Bible doesn't *condemn* borrowing. There are justifiable times (house, car, education, etc.) when a person needs up-front capital to obtain something that most people recognize as valuable in our culture. Understandably, those times need to be as few as possible and the loan obtained must be within reason. You can borrow money for legitimate reasons. At the same time, you need to balance this truth with the reality that there isn't one verse in the Bible that speaks *favorably* about debt. Not one! Every time you see the mention of debt, it's given with a negative connotation. With that in mind, I've chosen to concentrate on the area of consumer and credit card debt. Other debts like mortgage, business and investment debt are somewhat different, although the principles in this section can also apply to them.

The number of reasons people give for going into credit card and consumer debt are as many as the number of banks in the world that will offer them money; however, when you take all these explanations and boil them down to reality, there are four basic reasons why people go into some kind of consumer or credit card debt.

Some people go into long-term consumer borrowing because of greed. In our self-centered, materialistic world, too many people are concerned only about themselves and fulfilling their drive for self-gratification. Jesus warned about this kind of attitude when He said in Luke 12:15, *"Watch out! Be on your guard against all kinds of*

greed; a man's life does not consist in the abundance of his posses-
sions." When people go into long-term consumer and credit card
debt, sometimes it shows the avarice in their heart.

Perhaps one of the motives for this kind of compulsive drive is
what's known as the worldly "golden rule." *In other words, "He*
who has the gold rules." There are far too many people who think
that value and power are connected with material things. If you have
more "things," you have more worth and more influence. So they
love to swipe the plastic to get more. In their minds, the only things
in life that have value are the things *you can see and control.* So
they work under the premise that it's better to get it *now and handle*
the responsibilities of paying for it later.

How do you know if you're in this group? Take a look at your
consumer bills, especially clothing, entertainment, basic transportation and time spent eating out. Generally speaking, if you're not
able to stay within a monthly budget on any of these or other related
areas, chances are good that you want more than you can afford.
You don't have to buy the latest clothes to dress appropriately. Also,
you don't need to go to the trendiest restaurants to have a good time.
Remember this fact as well: a reliable used car will get you to the
same places as a brand new model—and at a cheaper price! The
issue revolves around your desires and wants. Are you over-paying
for your expensive tastes?

A second reason people go into long-term consumer debt is jeal-
ousy. This attitude is seen in the famous neighborhood proverb,
"Keeping up with the Jones." I know you've seen this throughout
your life. A neighbor across the street decides to get a new car. So
you must get a new car. He brings home a new riding lawn mower,
so you have to get a new riding lawn mower. Before you know it,
his house gets vinyl siding, so you have to get it on your home. And
on and on it goes. And with each effort to stay on the same level
with your neighbor, you go further and further into debt. This is
nothing more than sophisticated jealousy. The Tenth
Commandment was given not only to protect a person's property
from his neighbor's evil wishes, but also to expose his neighbor's
jealousy. When people borrow to keep up with others on the socio-
economic totem pole, it often shows the sinful envy in their heart.

Ananias and Sapphira's example in Acts 5 illustrates this principle. We learn from the first two verses that they sold a piece of property and gave a portion of the proceeds to the apostles. While this is commendable, keep in mind that the believers in that day shared *everything they possessed* (Acts 4:32). Ananias' example shows some signs of jealousy, especially in light of the fact that he lied to the apostles about the amount of money he obtained from the sale of the property. Perhaps there were some things he saw in his friends' lifestyles that he wanted in his own life. In any case, God's anger burned against him and it cost him his life along with his wife's life. Materialistic jealousy can keep you from becoming the kind of person God wants you to be.

How do you know if you're in this group? Evaluate your feelings when a friend, neighbor or classmate shows off something new before you. Does it make you want to get one too? Does motivation burn within you to keep up with others or to stay ahead of them? If you regularly find yourself trying to keep up with another person's status or social level, you're paying the daily price of emotional slavery.

A third reason people go into long-term consumer debt is fear. Perhaps you've seen the bumper sticker that expresses this truth. It says, "When the going gets tough, the tough go shopping." On its own, there's nothing wrong with shopping. However, some people go on shopping splurges to pick themselves up from a disappointing week or to bring temporary relief from a season of discouragement. Many of them will tell you that shopping brings temporary remission from the fears and troubles that bother them. So they go to the mall and buy. And their purchases take months to pay for everything that the plastic purchased in just seconds. Fear produces this urge to buy. And it reveals a lack of trust in God. Anxiety comes when we disbelieve that God can handle the needs of our life. Instead of turning to Him in faith and trust, we choose to satisfy our worries with physical things. And those physical things have a price tag clipped to them.

Jesus said in Matthew 6:31-33, "So do not worry, saying, 'What shall we eat?' or 'What shall we drink?' or 'What shall we wear?' For the pagans run after all these things, and your heavenly Father knows that you need them. But seek first His kingdom and His righteousness, and all these things will be given to you as well." I know from pastoral and personal experience that worry comes when I want to be in control instead of God. When I let Him take charge, He promises to give me His peace for my daily life.

How do you know if you're in this group? *Check the timing of your spending.* When do you buy things? Do you shop *before or after* you get your paycheck? Have you sat down and prepared a monthly budget? Do you know how much you can spend and what is "off limits?" *Many people don't realize the emotional bondage that comes when they charge something that they know they can't pay.* But they charge it anyway because of fear! They look for instantaneous pick-me-ups but those momentary gratifications bring long-term residual problems. As a result, they dig a deeper grave with every swipe of their plastic card.

Another common reason people go into long-term consumer debt is addiction. This is related to the above-mentioned cause of fear, but in my judgment it's more than fear. It comes from deep-seated insecurity. It's a habit of obtaining things to satisfy a problem rooted in a poor self-image. The people who fall into this cycle of addiction don't *want* to spend; they *have* to spend in order to feel good about themselves. They purchase excessive food, excessive clothes, expensive jewelry, cosmetics and other things to satisfy their addiction, and their purchases drive them deeper into debt. Poor self-image will drive people to all kinds of addictions: pornography, gambling, over-eating, alcohol and excessive spending to name just a few. These addictions are rooted in a deficient understanding of a person's uniqueness before God as well as insecurity in the value God places upon the individual.

This pattern of life raises the question of contentment and whether Christ can satisfy the deepest need of a person's heart. The apostle Paul understood that contentment could be found only in Christ. He wrote in Philippians 4:11-13, *"I am not saying this because I am in need, for I have learned to be content whatever the circumstances. I know what it is to be in need, and I know what it is to have plenty. I have learned the secret of being content in any and every situation, whether well fed or hungry, whether living in plenty or in want. I can do everything through Him who gives me strength."* At stake is the issue of personal satisfaction with Christ. Is He all that I really need? Or do I need something else to give me fulfillment?

How do you know if you're in this group? *Check your habits of spending.* How often do you feel a need to release tension with a swipe of the plastic? Do you spend money on things because you *need* them or because you simply have to spend? Evaluate the reasons for buying the clothes, food and household items that grace your home. Are they really necessary or are these purchases merely an escape?

You won't find positive statements from God about entering into long-term debt to satisfy your daily desires. The Bible says long-term consumer debt is bondage. In Proverbs 22:7 we read, *"The rich rule over the poor, and the borrower is servant to the lender."* Going into prolonged debt for things that provide temporary satisfaction brings extended misery and curses upon your life (Deuteronomy 28:43-45). In order to live with peace and freedom before God, you must learn how to get out of long-term consumer debt and make significant lifestyle decisions that will control your checkbook, your inner drives and your fears.

BASIC PRINCIPLES TO GET OUT OF LONG-TERM CONSUMER DEBT

Before I spend the next few pages outlining five basic principles for getting out of consumer debt, you need to know something about me, my wife and how we've used these truths in our own life and practice. I think it's important that you feel assured that you're reading from people who are truly experiencing the fruit of this biblical pattern. *These principles really work.* As of this writing, we've been married for close to 20 years. We have three teenage children not too far away from college. We're a typical American family, living in an average-sized home with a loyal black lab, a feisty white Bichon Frise and a finicky white cat. We have needs just like everyone has needs. But we built a solid biblical platform in our early adult financial life and it's paying off for us now. This platform centers on honoring God in all we do. Because the Lord is the creator of all good things (Psalm 103:1-5), we honor Him by working hard. Because we make obedience to Him the first priority in our life, He has chosen by His will to bless us on the promise of Matthew 6:33. We have seen that *because of these biblical principles and His promises, we don't live with consumer debt.* If there's a monthly bill, it's paid by the due date. Because of God's faithfulness in the stewardship of these biblical truths, both of our cars were paid with cash at the time of the sale. Keep in mind that in our early married years, most of this was done on an assistant pastor's compensation and my wife's part-time physical therapist's job. We don't make corporate big bucks and huge end-of-the-year bonuses! We say this to encourage you. *If these principles and promises can work for typical, average people like us, they'll work for you too! Put them to work!*

The first principle in getting out of long-term consumer debt is the process of hard examination. Look at your motives and habits for spending. This will take some time to do, so find some available hours when you can really focus on this step. Don't skip over it lightly! In many respects, it's one of the most important steps to do in reviewing your financial picture. It will provide the information you *really* need in order to make the right analysis of your situation. Here's what you do. Try to assemble all your checks, cash receipts and other expenditure records and lay them out on your kitchen table. *Take an honest, hard look at the way you spend money.* As you examine the facts, ask yourself some heart questions:

- What do I see? Are there any patterns of spending?
- Where does my paycheck go? Who gets it? Is this legitimate?
- How is my monthly income spent? Is this spending compulsive or planned? Do I jump to conclusions and spend money before it's earned?
- Why did I spend money on this? What were my motives?
- Did I have to spend this? Is this something I really need?

All too often, we don't take the proper time to ask ourselves some serious questions about our lifestyle habits. Why? Because our habits reflect the condition of our heart. Solomon wrote in Proverbs 4:23, *"Above all else, guard your heart, for it is the wellspring of life."* The outward habits of our life reflect the inward habits of our soul. If we're practicing undisciplined, compulsive spending on the outside, it reveals a disorganized, chaotic inner life. That's why a time of unbiased, critical examination is needed. If you're financially bleeding, you've got to stop the bleeding at the source. Look at the places where you and your spouse spend money. If you find that you can't do this practice alone, find a trusted friend, pastor or financial professional in your church and ask for help. Most people like to offer their help, provided you give them the proper information. Don't rush this procedure. Get a full, clear look. Make some conclusions and be prepared to accept them.

Let me make sure you understand something at this point. If you're married, it takes *both* husband and wife to review these financial figures and to accept the conclusions drawn from this examination. Don't let one partner do all the financial study and analysis, then report it to the other partner. *BOTH* partners need to look and to discuss the spending habits that are present in the household. You can't move forward to the next step *until you're in agreement* about the way you've spent money in the past. There must be a unified understanding about the realization of your financial picture and a mutually shared conviction about working together to find ways to get out of the red and to get into the black. Only when this is done can you move to the next step.

The second principle in getting out of long-term consumer debt is the process of conviction and confession. Now that you see your spending habits, what do they say about you? Are there some heart issues that need to be admitted and confessed? Are you in debt because of several compulsive decisions that were based on feelings, not facts? Did greed or jealousy plunge you into debt? Were you irresponsible in making a promise to pay for something, yet you didn't do it? Once you reach some factual conclusions in step one, go before the Lord in prayer and confess to Him your failures and misgivings. If you need to go to your spouse, other family members or others who are affected by your condition, *do it.* Seek by God's grace to deal with the heart attitudes that surface from your previous spending decisions. Make it your ambition to seek forgiveness from everyone affected by your former lifestyle.

Too many times, we fail to see the connection between our physical actions and our spiritual motives. *Going into long-term consumer debt shows lack of trust in God's provision for your life.* Paul told the Roman Christians, *"Everything that does not come from faith is sin"* (Romans 14:23b). The problem for too many people today is that they are not content with their present lifestyle. So they dig themselves an emotional grave with debt in order to obtain something that doesn't rightfully belong to them at this time. Compulsive debt shows selfishness, jealousy and greed, things that God despises. If these spiritual symptoms describe your present condition, you need to get things right with the Lord and with others affected. Never underestimate the power of forgiveness and a new start. As a great church leader once said, "The daily exercise of faith in Jesus Christ is a confession of sin."[54]

The third principle in getting out of long-term consumer debt is the process of simplification. Now that you're off to a new start with God and others, you need to reorganize your life and financial habits. This starts with simplifying your lifestyle. Paul's words to Timothy are helpful here: *"But godliness with contentment is great gain. For we brought nothing into the world, and we can take nothing out of it. But if we have food and clothing, we will be content with that. People who want to get rich fall into temptation and a trap and into many foolish and harmful desires that plunge men into ruin and destruction"* (1 Timothy 6:6-9). In application of this biblical truth, consider the following elements to simplify your lifestyle.

• ***Transportation***: Whatever you're driving, drive it *longer*, provided that it's paid for. There's an old saying, "The cheapest car to drive is the one you own." Most of the time, that's true with two exceptions. You should trade your present, paid car only if it becomes unsafe to drive or when the cost to repair it *exceeds* its fair market value. If you have an automobile that is digging you deeper into debt with high monthly payments and interest, *either sell it or trade it in for a lesser value car.* Too many irresponsible decisions are made with automobiles. If the bells and whistles of a new car appeal to you, *stay away from new car dealerships.* Visit or call a reputable used car lot and get them to work for you. Don't be lured into high monthly payments. Drive what your monthly budget can

---

[54] C.H. Spurgeon, "Honest Dealing with God," *Metropolitan Tabernacle Pulpit* (Pilgrim, 1971), Vol. 21, p. 367.

afford. Period!

• *Clothing*: Whatever you're wearing, *wear it longer.* You don't have to buy new outfits for every season of the year. *Buy only what you need for a period of time.* While you're limiting your clothing purchases during this time, pay off any department store clothing bills, then start putting aside monthly money in your family budget for clothes and shoes. Stretch your clothing and shoe money by timing your purchases during department store clearances and holiday sales, using newspaper coupons. Don't buy something the moment it comes out. Wait for it to go on clearance! While this is going on, keep many of your old clothes. Who knows? If you look at the way fashion designs work, they'll come *back* into style in a few years!

• *Housing*: Wherever you're living, *live in it a little longer.* Of course a possible exception to this is a rental home versus a purchased home situation. If you're renting an apartment for $500/month when you can own a home for the same monthly payment, it would most likely benefit you to buy the home, provided you plan to stay in it for at least 5 years and keep it in good shape. That situation is understandable. But if you currently own a home and are considering purchasing a bigger one, yet live with consumer debt, think about what you're doing. Do you really need a bigger house at this time? Have your family needs dramatically changed? Wouldn't it be better to remove those consumer debts *first* before you make a huge purchase like this? What's the current mortgage interest rate? Could you save more money refinancing your current home in order to pay off your consumer debts? If you're currently paying high interest credit card bills, take a realistic look at your housing situation before you decide to move to another home. As you're doing this, take a hard look at your utility bills. Is everyone cutting off their room lights when they leave? Is too much water wasted? Is your phone bill out of hand? *Look at your total housing situation.* The elimination of consumer debt must occupy the highest priority in your financial decisions. Don't take on more financial burdens until you eliminate your current obligations.

• *Food*: Pay careful attention to the things you place in your shopping cart. Plan your meals ahead of time on paper, using things that are advertised on sale at the grocery store. *Buy only what you need.* Use store, newspaper and on-line coupons to reduce your food costs.

Purchase generic brands; they're almost always lower than the national products (this also works for medicine). Watch carefully the red meat you purchase. You may fare better by purchasing cheaper meats like chicken, pork and turkey. *Shop only when you have a full stomach.* You won't be so easily tempted! By doing this, you can save money so that you can pay off some small monthly bills.

The fourth principle in getting out of long-term consumer debt is the act of production. You need to pray and to look for ways to earn *additional* money to pay off your debts as quickly as possible. For a period of time, you may need to ask your boss for some overtime hours. If that doesn't work, you may need to initiate some type of outside work (painting, lawn mowing, car cleaning and repair, computer help, bookkeeping, sewing, etc.) on weeknights or Saturdays so that during your "down time," you're generating extra money to eliminate your debts. Since many of the debts that people incur are based in laziness, Paul's words in 2 Thessalonians 3:10 ring strong: *"For even when we were with you, we gave you this rule: 'If a man will not work, he shall not eat."* Since you got yourself and your family into some financial problems, you need to work yourself out of them.

Take a moment and think of something you can do to earn extra money. What is it? Are you good with computers? Put a small ad in the paper for basic computer repair. Do you enjoy lawn mowing? This work pays BIG money these days! Ask my son. That's what he does for a summer job! Are you good at house painting or cleaning? That will earn respectable income these days. Another thing you can do in addition to work is *to sell something you currently own.* Look around your house and find any unused pieces of furniture, clothes, appliances or tools. Then have a big garage sale over the weekend. Put a yard sale ad in the classified section of the paper (some papers do this for free) and some signs near your home the day of the sale. Get the word out! There are many people who like these things, so be prepared to make some money for debt reduction! Get excited about paying off your debts while you simplify your possessions! There are many ways to generate more income. Think!

The fifth principle in getting out of long-term consumer debt is the commitment to generous, charitable giving. If you'll honor the Lord with your income by tithing, He will reward your heart motives and give you more in return. By "tithing," I mean giving ten percent of your income to your church as a part of your worship to the Lord. So many verses in the Bible testify to God's faithfulness to supply our needs when we put His kingdom *first* in our giving. Jesus said in Luke 6:38, *"Give and it will be given to you. A good measure, pressed down, shaken together and running over, will be poured into your lap. For with the measure you use, it will be measured to you."* Simply put, this passage talks about how the measure of giving comes back to us. If you give sparingly, you will receive sparingly. If you give generously, God returns a generous portion back to you. It's a matter of spiritual multiplication.

God has said that He will bless His people when they give generously, but He won't bless *until* they give. We must take the initiative. Proverbs 3 teaches us this principle clearly. So many times when we turn to this chapter, we immediately go to verses 5 and 6 to receive guidance and comfort from trusting the Lord. And that's good. But look at verse 9: *"Honor the Lord with your wealth, with the firstfruits of all your crops; THEN your barns will be filled to overflowing and your vats will brim over with new wine"* (my emphasis). Notice the order. When we honor God with generous giving, then (and only then) He comes with multiplied blessings. This is different than the "health and wealth" gospel. It's giving out of gratitude and obedience to God for what He has given us and will give us, not an automatic formula you use to get something from God after you've given Him your share. Giving is a matter of the heart from start to finish.

With this in mind, how's your giving these days? Do you tithe to your church? I've heard people tell me, "I can't afford to tithe." Listen to me clearly at this point. *You can't afford NOT to tithe.* If you were an employer and you knew your employees were stealing from you, what would you do? At the least, you would discipline them. In a similar way, if you fail to give to the Lord the full tithe, *the Bible says you're robbing Him* (Malachi 3:8-12). It could be that part of the reason you dug yourself into debt is because God withheld His blessing from your life because of your sin. Make a commitment TODAY to start giving to God what's due Him.

Let me take this thought to another level because I feel strongly about this principle. A number of years ago, I interviewed for a vacant pastoral position in a well-known church. During the interview, a godly man asked me if I tithed. "Sure," I said. Then he looked back at me and asked, "Are you happy with the income you're making these days?" I looked back at him with surprise and said, "I've never had anyone ask me a question like this, so I'll say, 'No' at this point. I have a family with three growing children. I could always use some more money." Then the hammer struck when he said, *"Why don't you tithe on what you want to make rather than on what you're currently earning?"* This thought blew my mind. Could it be true? Is this possible? So I tried it. Guess what? *IT WORKED!* Now keep this in mind. If you do this with the wrong motives, most likely it *won't work.* Why? Because God is testing your heart motives. On the other hand, if you do it over a period of time with godly intent, watch how God honors it. By tithing what you want to make, *you're sowing more seed into the Kingdom of God and Christ honors this.* So go on ahead—give it a try!

I can testify with great praise to God that He keeps His Word. If you honor Him, He chooses to bless you. I admit that it's a great mystery, but it's true. If you want to get out of debt, start examining your life and spending motives. Look at your heart. Confess your selfish habits. Simplify your lifestyle. Find ways to earn additional money to pay off your debts and give generously to the Lord in the journey. Remember Jesus' words, *"But seek first His kingdom and His righteousness, and all these things will be given to you as well."* He's ready to pull you out of the pit if you make some lifestyle decisions today.

SUMMARY

We've seen several reasons why money and possessions are significant to God. In addition to this, we've examined some of the most common reasons why people plunge into long-term consumer debt today. God has much to say in His Word regarding this kind of financial slavery. He has given us specific principles to get out of consumer debt and to enjoy the blessings of financial independence in our daily lives. But it takes planning, hard work, discipline, simplification and a commitment to generous giving in order to experience these rewards. Are you willing to take God at His Word? Is the time right to look honestly at your finances? Do you have too much? Are you tithing?

THINK ABOUT THIS

One of the best books I've ever read on this subject is *Money, Possessions and Eternity* by Randy Alcorn. Ponder his insightful words for a while.

> If all evangelical Christians were out of debt, countless millions of dollars could be freed up for the Kingdom of God. Our families would also be stronger, since surveys indicate that financial pressures caused by indebtedness are a major factor in more than half of all divorces. We speak with disdain of the national debt and politicians who cannot limit their spending to available revenues. But the truth is, our national debt is simply an extension of the same irresponsible mentality that many of us consistently demonstrate in our own financial dealings. Home mortgages, auto loans, credit cards—all are normal to us, but debt evokes severe warnings from God's Word. We must take a closer look at the phenomenon of debt to understand the underlying problem it presents to the Christian.[55]

PRAYER

Heavenly Father, I realize that the way I handle money shows the spiritual condition of my heart. Forgive me for the times when I failed to be a proper steward of Your resources. Today I repent of my greed, jealousy and selfishness and ask You to fill me with the Holy Spirit's security and confidence. Give me wisdom to look at my finances and to do whatever is necessary to get out of debt as quickly as possible. Help me to simplify my lifestyle. Help me to learn contentment. Most of all give me a generous giving spirit. Help me to do with it a happy heart. In all my financial affairs, may

---

[55] *Money, Possessions and Eternity*, p. 310.

the Lordship of Christ be present for all to see. In Your Great Name I pray. AMEN.

TALK TIME!

1. Does it surprise you that 15% of all the recorded words of Jesus dealt in one way or another with money and possessions?
2. Review the accounts of Zacchaeus (Luke 19) and the rich young ruler (Matthew 19). How does Christ view the use of money in the world?
3. Discuss this sentence: "Your attitude toward money and possessions tell others what you think is important in this world."
4. Review the reasons why people go into long-term consumer debt. Are any reasons particularly true with you? How are you dealing with it?
5. Go back and examine the principles needed to get out of consumer debt. Which step is the hardest for you? Which one will be the easiest?
6. How hard is it to simplify your lifestyle? What are some real ways you can do this?
7. Comment on this sentence: "You can't afford NOT to tithe." Do you believe it? Are you practicing this biblical principle?
8. Do you know someone who is struggling with debt? How can this lesson equip you to help him/her?

PART 3:

HELP IN THE MIDST OF THE TENSION

13

PROMISES THAT GOVERN MY LIFE

"Through these He has given us His very great and precious promises, so that through them you may participate in the divine nature and escape the corruption in the world caused by evil desires."
2 Peter 1:4

In his great work, *Pilgrim's Progress*, John Bunyan tells of a time when Christian left the main road to follow another path that appeared easier. Unfortunately, this trail led him to the region of Giant Despair who owned Doubting Castle.

Giant Despair captured Christian and placed him in a dungeon. He told Christian to forget his journey and consider suicide. From all outward appearances, it looked like the end of the line for Christian; however, Christian's companion Hope started to remind him of his previous victories. So they prayed in a spirit of intercession until almost the break of morning. It was then that Christian realized he had a significant treasure in his possession. With passion in his heart, he said:

> What a fool am I thus to lie in a stinking dungeon,
> when I may as well be at liberty. I have a key in
> my bosom called promise that will, I am persuaded,
> open any lock in Doubting Castle.[56]

---

[56] John Bunyan, *Pilgrim's Progress* (Moody, no date given), p. 136.

Hope looked back at him and said, "That's good news. Good brother, pluck it out of thy bosom and try." And the prison gates flew open when the Key of Promise was inserted.

Over the course of this work, we've examined a number of significant tension areas that plague people in their daily lives. We've also seen how God offers significant daily help when you really need it. I hope that you'll review these chapters and let the truths of God's Word equip you as you seek to gain help and hope for the days ahead. God stands ready to strengthen you and to lift you above these problems, provided you turn to Him in repentance and in surrender.

But sometimes it's just plain tough to handle the daily pains of life's bumps and bruises. While you're feeling the pain of these troubles and heartaches, is there something you can claim? While you're undergoing the hurt and worry of bad decisions, difficult children, debt, discouragement, confusion and overload in your work and marriage, is there something you can hold on to that can give you some perspective and relief? In my life, I've experienced some tremendous mountain peak experiences. I've also bled from bitter times in the valley. When doubt, discouragement and frustration try to overtake me, I've found some important promises in the Bible that have given me significant help in getting through these valley experiences with a sane mind and a strong heart. These promises are dear to me and have kept me going at times when everything else has gone sour.

The following promises regularly remind me that God is in control and that He has reasons for the circumstances and timing of my life. When I've really needed Him the most, He has shown *that no matter how tough the road may be, there is help along the way as you journey to the end.* I'm going to place these promises in priority so that you can see the order and natural progression that flows from one to the other. When you're in the midst of some dark, hard times, look at the things God wants you to know!

GOD'S PLANS

The first promise that gives me hope and encouragement is the knowledge that God has a plan for my life. The Lord spoke these

204

words through the Prophet Jeremiah: *"For I know the plans I have for you, declares the Lord, plans to prosper you and not to harm you, plans to give you hope and a future. Then you will call upon me and come and pray to me, and I will listen to you. You will seek me and find me when you seek me with all your heart"* (Jeremiah 29:11-13). When I'm experiencing times of hurt, defeat or general despair, I always fall back on the promise that God has a plan for my life. *He has a plan for your life!* These plans are intended to give you hope and a bright future. You and I can rest in the confidence that God doesn't make mistakes. Our lives aren't accidents. God knows what He's doing!

This promise has helped me at times when I've gotten bad news in a letter or phone call or when a friend betrayed my confidence to another person. These kinds of things don't catch God by surprise. So when times like these happen and you're hurt, don't look up and say, "God, look at the mess I'm in" and expect Him to say, "Why, I didn't know that! Thanks for telling me!" The truth is that God many times takes the initiative to break into our world with these kinds of things to catch our attention and to force us to think. *He has to put some people on their back in order for them to look up.* Are you one of these people? Think about your place in life right now. If you're lying in a puddle of doubt, why not admit to Him your questions and ask how your position fits with His plans for your life?

GOD'S PURPOSES

Once we realize that God has a plan for our lives, we can understand to a better degree that the things we experience in our daily journey happen for specific purposes. *This leads us to the second promise that God has a purpose for our lives.* Bible teachers and theologians refer to this as "the end that justifies the means" promise. It's based in principle on the words of Romans 8:28, *"And we know that in all things God works for the good of those who love Him, who have been called according to His purpose."* If God's end is for His character to shine through my life, He'll place experiences in my daily walk that will reveal His good and perfect will. He uses these life events much like a carpenter uses a sharp chisel to shape a block of wood on a high-speed lathe. As we allow Him to carve

His Holy Spirit into our daily trials and struggles, He conforms and shapes us more and more to the image of Jesus Christ in our spiritual lives.

If you have children, a good way to illustrate this promise is to bake a cake from scratch. Put out all the ingredients you'll need to prepare a bowl of cake batter for the oven. Show your children the baking soda, baking powder, flour and all the other elements of the recipe. Ask them, "would you like to taste the baking powder? How about sampling a raw egg?" Care to put some flour in your mouth?" Of course none of them want to taste any of these elements *individually* but blend them together and you have the makings of a great cake! With that in mind, drive home the point with this thought. *Let these recipe elements symbolize God's purposes.* We see some of them in the cake batter, but others we don't. But they're all there! Now drive home this important point. At times we get stuck in our own quagmires and we can't see the end. We question God and say, "Why did this happen? What's the purpose behind this event?" It's in those times when God is silent that we most need to trust His purposes. He knows our dilemma and He has reasons for it. I can trust Him not only with the end, but also with the means to that end.

God's Priorities

The third promise that gives me hope and encouragement is the realization that God will supply my daily needs when I put His Kingdom first. In my earlier years, I worried too much. I think part of it was due to the fact that I didn't see (or sometimes I didn't want to see) God's plans and purposes for my life. Jesus' words in Matthew 6:33 are God's answer to the daily worries that drag us down: *"But seek first His kingdom and His righteousness, and all these things will be given to you as well."* The promise is real. If God is going to take care of the lilies of the field and feed the birds of the air, He'll take care of you and me in the process.

But the promise goes further than this. It states that if we focus on God's business, *He'll take care of our business.* If we make His Kingdom our top priority, then He'll supply the things in life that we *truly need.* This parallels the famous saying, "God's work, done God's way, will have God's resources." If your desire in life is to delight in the Lord, the Bible says that He will give you the desires of your heart (Psalm 37:4). Could it be that the reason some people struggle with worry, debt and their future is because they were first concerned about themselves and not about God's Kingdom? Is it possible that they are reaping now what they sowed years ago? Let Galatians 6:8 answer this powerfully: *"The one who sows to please his sinful nature, from that nature will reap destruction; the one who sows to please the Spirit, from the Spirit will reap eternal life."* Like my dad always told me, "Son, the more of heaven there is in your life, the less of earth you need to covet." How true!

GOD'S PATHS

The fourth promise that gives me hope and encouragement is the knowledge that God gives meaning to life when you put your trust in Him. Proverbs 3:5-6 says, *"Trust in the Lord with all your heart and lean not on your own understanding; in all your ways acknowledge Him, and He will make your paths straight."* As we walk down the road of life, we're confronted with issues and decisions that are extremely difficult and confusing. When we put God *first* in our life and seek His glory in everything we do, He promises to lead us step by step, moment by moment in His will. His Word assures us that if we trust Him during the times when we need Him the most, He promises to give us meaning on our journey that is both real and satisfying.

Several years ago when I was preaching at a Sunday night service on discerning God's guidance, an older gentleman in the church came to me after the closing prayer and handed me a seasoned piece of paper that was stuck in his Bible for many years. On this crumbled paper were the following words by Andrew Murray:

Believer! Would you abide in Jesus, let it be day by day...God has gathered up the moments and bound them up into a bundle, for the very purpose that we might take measure of them. As we look forward in the morning, or look back in the evening, and weigh the moments, we learn how to value and how to use them rightly. And even as the Father, with each new morning, meets you with the promise of just sufficient manna for the day for yourself and those who have to partake with you, meet Him with the bright and loving renewal of your acceptance of the position He has given you in His beloved Son...Let each day have its value from your calling to abide in Christ.[57]

GOD'S PROVISIONS

The fifth promise that gives me hope and encouragement is the realization that what you give to God comes back to you in measure. Luke 6:38 says, *"Give, and it will be given to you. A good measure, pressed down, shaken together and running over, will be poured into your lap. For with the measure you use, it will be measured to you."* There is so much breadth and power in this verse that it's hard to appreciate its full implications. Because it's meaning is so explosive, some people have refused to make it a strategic promise for their lives. They do this to their own loss, not realizing the power and freedom that it can bring to their inner life.

In effect, what Jesus says in this verse is incredible. He simply teaches that when you give to God, God gives back to you. But there's something more. *In God's investment world, the proportion of your giving equals the return of His blessing.* If you give much, He returns much. If you give little, He returns little. When you measure out your giving, the Lord sees the dimensions of your faith. With these parameters in His sight, He then converts them to His scale and sends a blessing back to you in some form. Sometimes the form of blessing is a daily monetary provision. Other times it's the prevention of a terrible calamity that could have wiped you out either physically or financially. Perhaps the blessing is a provision that is greater than what you expected. It could also be a prolonged endurance of something that *should* have stopped or died a long time ago (car, freezer, etc.). Whatever form the blessing comes, it reveals the measure of God's faithfulness in proportion to the faith you show in Him.

This truth was powerfully impressed upon my life as a child dur-

---

[57] Andrew Murray, *Abide in Christ* (Whitaker House, 1979), p. 95.

ing my church's annual Vacation Bible School. Mary Rose, a godly woman who taught me some of the most memorable lessons a child could ever learn, brought three spoons to illustrate the truth of this verse. The first spoon was a baby-feeding spoon. I remember how tiny it looked and how little it could hold. She said there were many people who gave to God that way. *They were stingy and cheap.* As a result, they got little in return.

The second spoon she displayed was a serving spoon. It looked like something you would find in a casserole dish on a serving table. It could put a proportionate amount of food on your plate. She likened this spoon to people that gave a tithe (10% gross) to the Lord's work. *They were obedient, yet measurement-minded people.* They did what was right and honorable in the Lord's eyes. Because of their proportions, they got something back in return.

But the third spoon caught my attention. It was the biggest punch bowl ladle I'd ever seen. She dipped it into a big tub of water, then poured the water from the ladle into a glass. Guess what? The glass couldn't hold all of the water! It poured over the top! Holding everyone spellbound, she asked, "If you've got a lot of glasses to fill, what kind of spoon do you want?" Without thinking, all of us chose the big ladle. Then she drove home the lesson. *"If you give generously to God with unlimited measure, God will pour it back to you—AND MORE!"* Her teaching point was to illustrate the *measures* of faith that were seen in different people. In God's mind, it's not an eye for an eye or a dollar for a dollar. *It's your measure against God's measure.* If what you give measures out significantly to the Lord, He'll measure a proportionate blessing in return. With this Vacation Bible School lesson impressed upon my mind, I remember going to the playground asking myself the question, "Does my giving look like a baby spoon, a serving spoon or a big ladle?" How about you?

GOD'S PERSEVERANCE

The sixth promise that gives me hope and encouragement is the understanding that whatever's hitting me these days, I need to hang in there a little longer and watch God work. From a human perspective, this is commonly called persevering. From a divine perspective, it's God's holding and keeping power when you feel you can't go on. You see this promise in Hebrews 10:36, *"You need to persevere so that when you have done the will of God, you will receive what He has promised."* All of us understand that much of life is a struggle. Sometimes the Lord engineers these struggles so that our faith and spiritual life will grow. Sometimes we put ourselves through these conflicts from our own immaturity and ignorance. In either case, the important thing to remember about these struggles in life is that they are lessons in the arena of perseverance. We need to rest in the strength of God's grace and to hold to His hope because this promise is real. *If you do His will, you will receive what He has promised you.* So whatever's attacking your patience, challenging your faith and pulling you down, remember God's promise. Hang in there! Obey God's will and watch what He's going to do in you and through you.

I have several prized objects in my office that remind me of this promise regularly. One is the singing "Big Mouth Billy Bass" that my daughter gave me for Christmas. One of the songs it sings is "Don't Worry, Be Happy."[58] I push the red button on that fish almost daily to remind me of this simple truth. There's no practical value in worrying even when struggle marks my day. Rest in God's grace and enjoy the contentment that He wants to give.

Two additional wall hangings remind me to hang in there a little longer. Below a picture of a runner are the words, *"DETERMINA-TION: The race is not always to the swift...But to those who keep on running."* Right beside it is another picture that says,

"THE FOUNDATION OF EXCELLENCE:
Tentative efforts lead to tentative outcomes. Therefore give yourself fully to your endeavors. Decide to construct your character through excellent actions and determine to pay the price of a worthy goal. The trials you encounter will introduce you to your strengths. Remain stead-fast...and one day you will build something that endures;

---

[58] "Don't Worry, Be Happy" by Bobby McFerrin (© 1988, Prob Noblem Music).
[59] Epictetus, Roman teacher and philosopher (55-135 AD). Both quotations are on wall hangings made by Successories (800) 926-5724.

something worthy of your potential." 59

Those words didn't come from the Bible, but they're God's truth. Persistence, faithfulness and determination are qualities that God wants to develop within us. Whatever you're grappling with these days, stick with it! Persevere and watch what God will do in you, through you and around you for His glory. He's introducing you to something incredible down the road!

SUMMARY

God is truly there when we need Him the most! He has some wonderful promises for us no matter how tough the road gets at times. He has a great *plan* for your life! Many times He puts circumstances, events and people in our paths to reveal His *purposes* for our daily journey. But when we make His Kingdom our top *priority*, He will supply our human and spiritual needs according to His gracious word. When we trust Him with all our heart, He will guide and direct our *paths* in life. When we give generously by faith in love to Him, He gives back to us according to His measured *provisions*. No matter how difficult your struggles may appear today, hang in there! When you've done His will through *perseverance*, you will receive these and many other precious promises from His merciful hand. Let these closing words from 1 Corinthians 2:9 give you hope as you go out to face the daily struggles of your life:

No eye has seen, no ear has heard, no mind has conceived what God has prepared for those who love Him.

PRAYER

Heavenly Father, I'm grateful to know that You have all kinds of incredible promises for my life. You've been there for me every time I've needed You. Forgive me for the times I've strayed from Your presence and Your direction. I confess my sin, my ignorance and immaturity in failing to stay close to you. Today, I'm making a new commitment to follow Your ways and plans for my life. Thank you for wanting to be a part of my daily activities. I need You now more than ever. I ask You to empower me to overcome worry, fear, overload and confusion. Give me the strength of Your Holy Spirit to accept my past failures and to rest in Your restorative grace. I'm making You the center of my marriage and my home. Help me to love my spouse the way You love him/her. Pour out Your love through me to my children. I claim the promises in Your Word and ask that You use them to build faith in me. I want to be a trophy of Your amazing grace in this world. Thank you for what You're going to do in my life in the days to come. In Your precious and wonderful Name I pray. AMEN.

TALK TIME!

1. How comforting is it to know that God has some great promises for your life? Of the six promises mentioned, which one do you need the most today? Why?
2. Discuss this sentence: "Once we realize that God has a plan for our lives, we can better understand that the things we experience in our daily journey happen for specific purposes."
3. Why is it so hard to "seek first God's Kingdom and righteousness" (Matthew 6:33) at times? What are some of the things that keep us from experiencing this truth?
4. Comment on the cake illustration and its relationship to Romans 8:28. Care to try it?
5. Read Luke 6:38 and discuss the three spoons illustration. What spoon do you think best represents most professing Christians today? Which one describes you?
6. Discuss this thought: "The proportion of your giving equals the return of God's blessing."
7. Do you know someone who needs encouragement in the promises of God today? How can this lesson equip you to help him/her?

WHEN I NEED GOD THE MOST
Final Thoughts

As a pastor, I've seen on a daily basis among professing believers a constant battle over a group of "tension areas" in their personal lives. Struggles such as confusion, doubt, discouragement, failure, worry, guidance, work, burnout, marriage, rearing children and debt have paralyzed the minds and hearts of many Christians who want to glorify God in their life but struggle through the week with little victory.

There have been several good books written in the past few years that cover each of the above areas thoroughly; however in my experience, I've discovered that many people have a *number* of these problems and tensions in their life; not just one or two. Chances are good that if you've got doubt, you're also struggling with worry, burnout, discouragement, family tensions and fears of failure. With the multiplicity of tension points attacking every day, the probability of buying four or five books, each covering a specific tension point, is financially unfeasible and not practical. As a result, many believers don't purchase anything, remaining in a quagmire of defeat and discouragement.

When I Need God the Most is an introductory series of Bible Studies geared to equip believers to understand the practical biblical help that is available to them from the Lord when they encounter tough times in their life. This work is not intended to replace any of the deeper studies and current works out in the market. Rather, it's intended to serve as an introduction to the common problems that many people face today. After reading this work, believers can better search for additional help in the areas they feel they need deeper assistance. Plus the added bonus of studying this book in a group setting (Home or Office Bible study, Sunday School class) can equip believers to minister to one another with these problems.

THIS RESOURCE IS IDEAL FOR:

- Sunday School Classes (13 lessons for a Sunday School quarter).

213

- Weekly small group Bible studies with *TALK TIME!* discussion questions at the end of each chapter.
- Felt need support groups.
- Outreach for believers to unbelievers (since it deals with areas that unbelievers as well as believers struggle with on a daily basis).
- Pastors, teachers, church laymen and laywomen and people in general who come into contact with hurting and struggling people on a weekly basis.

LAMP AND LIGHT CLUB

"YOUR WORD IS A LAMP TO MY FEET AND A LIGHT
TO MY PATH"
–PSALM 119:105

MONTHLY IN-DEPTH BIBLE STUDY AND EXPOSITION MINISTRY

Scripture exhorts us, "Do your best to present yourself to God as one approved, a workman who does not need to be ashamed and who correctly handles the word of truth" (2 Timothy 2:15).

Lamp and Light Resources exist to equip everyday lay people, pastors and growing Christians to study the Word of God on a richer, deeper level. Monthly lessons are prepared to equip believers with a deeper understanding of God's Word with fresh application to today's living.

By enrolling in this monthly Bible study and exposition club, you will receive:
• 2 in-depth Bible lessons on 1 cassette tape each month.
• Helpful study guide outlines suited for notebook storage and review
• Guided instruction that's easy to understand and to apply
• Offers on special Bible study resources at discount prices

ENROLL TODAY—JUST $8.95 A MONTH FOR 2 STUDIES!

Sign up on the next page!

Name _____

Address _____

City_____ State_____ Zip _____

E-mail _____

Credit Card _____

Number _____

Expires_____ / _____

Name as it appears on your credit card

_____

Signature _____

Mail to: Lamp and Light Resources
                  P.O. Box 30934
                  Clarksville, TN 37040

                  **You can also enroll by logging on to
                  www.lampnlight.com**